PRAYER-BASED GROWTH GROUPS

PRAYER-BASED GROWTH GROUPS

•

Charles F. Kemp

ABINGDON PRESS
NASHVILLE • NEW YORK

PRAYER-BASED GROWTH GROUPS

Library of Congress Cataloging in Publication Data

KEMP, CHARLES F   1912-
Prayer-based growth groups.
Bibliography: p.
1. Church group work.   2. Prayers.   I. Title.
BX652.2.K45   248   74-11174

ISBN 0-687-33369-5

Scripture quotations noted RSV are from the Revised Standard Version of the Bible, copyright 1946, 1952, and 1971 by the Division of Christian Education, National Council of Churches, and are used by permission.

Acknowledgments are made to the following publishers:

Abingdon Press for a prayer from *Songs from the Slums* by Toyohiko Kagawa, copyright renewal 1963 by Lois J. Erickson, used by permission of the publisher; and for a prayer from *Lift Up Your Hearts* by Walter Russell Bowie, copyright © 1939, 1956 by Pierce and Washabaugh (Abingdon Press).
Association Press for a prayer reprinted by permission from *The Student Prayerbook* by John Oliver Nelson, Association Press, Publisher.
E. P. Dutton & Co. and J. M. Dent and Sons for a prayer from the book *The Temple* by W. E. Orchard. Copyright 1918 by E. P. Dutton & Co., Inc. Renewal, 1946, by W. E. Orchard. Published by E. P. Dutton & Co., Inc., and J. M. Dent and Sons, Ltd., and used with their permission.
Harper & Row, Publishers, Inc., for a prayer (p. 7) in *The Daily Altar*, edited by Herbert L.Willett and Charles Clayton Morrison (Harper & Row); and for a prayer from pp. 12-13 in *A Book of Public Prayers* by Harry Emerson Fosdick, copyright © 1959 by Harry Emerson Fosdick. Reprinted by permission of the publisher.
Harper & Row, Publishers, Inc., and William Collins Sons, for excerpts from pp. 88, 20, 66, 57, and entire prayer "In The Morning" (p. 20) from *A Guide to Daily Prayer* by William Barclay (British title, *More Prayers for the Plain Man*). Copyright © 1962 by William Barclay. By permission of the publishers.
Holt, Rinehart and Winston, Inc., and William Heinemann Ltd., for a prayer from *Are You Running with Me, Jesus?* by Malcolm Boyd. Copyright © 1965 by Malcolm Boyd. Reprinted by permission of the publishers.
Charles Scribner's Sons for two prayers by Reinhold Niebuhr from *Prayers for Services* by Morgan Phelps Noyes. Copyright 1934 Charles Scribner's Sons. Reprinted by permission of the publisher.

MANUFACTURED BY THE PARTHENON PRESS AT
NASHVILLE, TENNESSEE, UNITED STATES OF AMERICA

Contents

III. Appendixes

Introduction

THE ORIGIN OF THE IDEA

In days such as these we need all the resources we can get. Anything that will help us understand ourselves better, or the religious life more, should be considered. This manual describes a type of spiritual growth group that is uniquely suited to a church setting. It is based on a study of the great prayers of the faith and a sharing of reactions to them.

The ideas and procedures discussed here developed gradually. They came about quite unexpectedly, even unsought. A description of how this plan evolved might make clearer the descriptions and suggestions in the book.

POETRY THERAPY

I was assigned the responsibility of supervising a graduate thesis on the use of poetry therapy in pastoral counseling. I knew nothing about poetry therapy and didn't really want to learn. It sounded to me as if it would be evading real issues and could result in a vague sort of sentimentalism. However, in order to be familiar with the project my student was pursuing, I began to explore some of the literature on the subject.

One of the better publications was a book edited by Jack J. Leedy entitled *Poetry Therapy* (Lippincott, 1969). It included contributions by several authors, all of whom had used poetry therapy very effectively with very difficult cases, including disturbed adolescents, and patients in mental hospitals.

The procedures were quite simple. The therapist, or leader, would read a poem to the group, and then the group would respond. The therapists found that some persons would respond to the mood and the thought of the poet and reveal needs and dynamics that had not been discovered by more conventional forms of diagnosis and therapy.

Poets speak a universal language, free from all technical terms and jargon. They lay bare their own souls; they share their moods, their attitudes, and their feelings. People, especially people under stress, are able to identify with some of these moods and thus find it easier to express their own.

Patients would sometimes discuss the lives of the poets as well as the content of their poems. This had an additional value. It was encouraging to know that even some famous, creative persons had experienced the same or similar conflicts and anxieties. By identifying with them, the patient gained a new hope and source of strength.

Dr. Leedy, who is director of the Poetry Therapy Center in New York City, encourages his patients to read poetry aloud and to experiment with writing their own poetry. Reading aloud helps them to respond more directly to the mood of the poem, which, he feels, increases its healing effect. Writing their own poems helps them gain insight into their own feelings and provides him with another diagnostic tool or means of evaluation.

All in all, the advocates of poetry therapy listed many practical therapeutic values. They found it helped make their patients' difficulties easier to bear; it hastened their recovery; it helped them develop a philosophy of life; it encouraged them to explore their feelings, often at a deeper level than they had done before; it extended their emotional range; it helped them find patterns of control, it led to experiences of self-fulfillment; it enabled them to identify with others and to gain deeper insights into themselves.

When reading the book, the thought occurred to me, If this is true of poetry, why should it not be true of prayer? I reread some of the chapters with prayer in mind. Poetry speaks of universal experiences, but so does prayer. This raised several questions.

If the words of great poems make emotional disorders easier to bear, help develop a philosophy of life, encourage persons to explore their feelings, develop hope, and attain fulfillment, why not the use of great prayers?

If persons can identify with the conflicts, anxieties, and concerns of the poets and gain from them hope and courage, why could they not identify with the feelings, anxieties, and conflicts of men of prayer and gain from them hope and trust?

If discussing the content of poems leads to insight and understanding and broadens one's outlook, why shouldn't the discussion of some of the great prayers of courage and faith do the same thing?

If there is value in knowing and discussing the lives of some of the great poets, why should one not find the same value in discussing the lives of some of the great men and women of faith?

If poetry can encourage a person to express himself by creating his own poems and can help him to verbalize his own feelings, why couldn't the great prayers stimulate and guide a person to phrase his own prayers and lead to a new and deeper expression of prayer?

PRAYER:
A RECORD OF MAN'S STRIVING

These thoughts led naturally to a second step: the study of prayers. Not a study of prayer. I had done that many times. I had read Herman, von Hügel, Fosdick, Buttrick, Underhill, and many others who had written about prayer. This was different. This was a study of prayers themselves. It proved to be a most interesting and rewarding experience.

A study of prayers covers a wide range. It includes all generations, all races, all cultures. It crosses all geographical, denominational, and theological lines. It includes prayers as recorded in Scripture, in the devotional classics, in biographies and journals, in hymns and poetry, in ancient liturgy, and in contemporary collections and anthologies.

It has been said that prayer is the "heart of religion." If this is true, then it follows that one of the best ways to study religion, or the spiritual life, is to study prayers.

In prayer we have a record of man's striving.

There is a striving after wisdom, such as Solomon's prayer when he became king of Israel, generations before the time of Christ: "Give thy servant therefore an understanding mind to govern thy people" (1 Kings 3:9 RSV). Centuries after Christ, Abraham Lincoln said, "I have been driven many times to my knees by the overwhelming conviction I had nowhere else to go. My own wisdom and that of all about me seemed insufficient for the task."

There is a striving to overcome guilt and to be assured of forgiveness, as in these words of the psalmist:

> Have mercy on me, O God
>   according to thy steadfast love;
> according to thy abundant mercy
>   blot out my transgressions.
> Wash me thoroughly from my iniquity,
>   and cleanse me from my sin!
>   (Psalm 51:1-2 RSV)

Similar thoughts are expressed in Augustine's *Confessions*.

There is a striving for understanding and commitment, as when St. Francis knelt in the chapel of St. Damian and prayed, "Shed Thy light, I beseech Thee, into the darkness of my mind, and so be found in me that I may do all things in accordance with Thy holy will."

There is a striving for growth, which Louis Untermeyer expressed in his prayer, complete in one sentence: "Lord, keep me forever dissatisfied."

There is a search for serenity, which is reflected in

Whittier's poem/prayer that has found its way into our hymnbooks:

> Drop thy still dews of quietness,
> Till all our strivings cease;
> Take from our souls the strain and stress,
> And let our ordered lives confess
> The beauty of thy peace.

There is a striving after humility, which is stressed over and over both in the general passages and in the prayers in Thomas a Kempis' *Imitation of Christ.*

There is a striving for courage, as when Luther prayed, "Do Thou, my God, stand by me, against all the world"; or when E. B. Pusey prayed, "Most loving Lord, give me a childlike love of Thee, which may cast out all fear."

There is a striving for faith, as when the father of the sick boy said to Jesus, "I believe; help my unbelief"; or as when Henry Ward Beecher prayed from his pulpit, "We beseech of Thee, grant us this faith, that shall give us victory over the world and over ourselves."

Sources for the further study of prayers are given on pages 28-37 and in the Bibliography.

SPIRITUAL GROWTH GROUP

The next step was one of experimentation: an attempt to combine the methods and ideas used in poetry therapy with the deep spiritual resources found in the prayers of the Christian faith.

I was somewhat familiar with what Clyde Reid in *Groups Alive—Church Alive* calls "the small group explosion." I read some of the literature on the small-group movement in order to apply the principles found there to the development of a spiritual growth group based on historical and contemporary expressions of prayer.

I did not have in mind a prayer group in the traditional sense, but one that would use the prayers of others as a means for both personal and religious understanding and as a guide and stimulus for spiritual growth. This was a different kind of group from any I found described in the literature. It was also one that seemed especially suitable for church groups.

The next step was to experiment with groups and to suggest to others that they do likewise. We have had experiences that have convinced us that such a program has real value. The principles and procedures we have followed and some of the material that has been prepared as the basis for discussion comprise the remainder of this manual.

I
METHODS
AND PROCEDURES

The next six chapters describe how the use of prayer in spiritual growth groups has been applied experimentally and suggest how other groups could follow the same principles. These are only suggestions. The whole idea is subject to a wide variety of procedures and offers many opportunities for creative adaptation.

THE NEED AND VALUE OF A SPIRITUAL GROWTH GROUP

A young professional man whom we once knew wanted to discuss a problem. He was dissatisfied with his religion. He was not agnostic or critical. He was not neurotic or maladjusted. He was not guilty of anything immoral or illegal. He was a good churchman. He attended worship, participated in an adult program of religious education, paid his pledge, served on boards and committees. He simply felt that there should be more to his religious life than he had yet achieved. He felt there were possibilities he had not realized.

In his book *Groups Alive—Church Alive* (p. 74), Clyde Reid tells of another man who was also a good churchman. He states his problem to his pastor this way: "Some of us feel the need for a deeper spiritual pilgrimage. We just don't find that on Sunday mornings, and ushering doesn't satisfy this hunger. Teaching Sunday school doesn't seem to do it either. We'd like to start a new group and we need your help. Could you meet with some of us on Friday night?"

These two men expressed a common concern, namely, the need to grow. They were normal people who were aware of potentials, but also aware they hadn't yet attained them.

It is people such as these that we have in mind in this study. A spiritual growth group is designed specifically to meet their need. Before continuing perhaps we should define what a spiritual growth group is.

There is no shortage of groups available today. The small-group movement has been one of the sociological phenomena of recent years. All over the country have appeared a vast number and many varieties of groups: encounter groups, therapy groups, T. A. groups, sensitivity groups, groups to discuss certain topics, groups to meet specific needs. While the mushrooming of groups is a contemporary phenomenon, the idea is very old, especially within the church. The Wesleyan prayer meeting in the early days of Methodism, the Oxford movement, the traditional Sunday school class with its programs of study and fellowship, Quaker sessions of silence, all were religiously oriented small groups.

Much can be said for the fact that the New Testament church consisted primarily of small informal groups that met for mutual support and growth.

Many of the churches described in Paul's letters, for example, met in homes, shared meals, united in prayer and worship.

The spiritual growth group as conceived here does not take the place of any existing activities of the church. Rather it is seen as something in addition to traditional programs of education, service, and worship. Religious growth groups can take many forms and have many expressions. Howard Clinebell, in his helpful little book on growth groups entitled *The People Dynamic* (pp.11-12), lists twenty-three different kinds of growth groups. No doubt there are many others.

Simply stated, a spiritual growth group is a small group of people who are seeking to attain growth in their understanding of religion and in religious experiences which should also result in growth in personal awareness and self-fulfillment. The type of growth group described here has the same purposes as any growth group. It is unique in that it centers its focus on some of the great prayers of the church past and present.

Perhaps it would help to state some of the things such a group isn't. It is not a social group, although it may experience some things that are genuinely enjoyable, and create an atmosphere which results in fellowship and friendship at its deepest level. It is not an educational group, although much learning may take place. This may include information about religion and life in general, but, even more important, one may learn much about oneself. It is not a therapy group, although much that is therapeutic may take place. Howard Clinebell distinguishes between growth groups and therapy groups this way:

"The growth orientation is the guiding perspective; the emphasis is more on unused potential, here-and-now effectiveness in living, and future goals —than on past failures, problems, and pathology" (*The People Dynamic*, p. 3).

This does not mean problems are ignored. Some may be faced, discussed, even eliminated. Some may be resolved or reduced by the principle of incompatibilities. Tension and relaxation, for example, are incompatible. One cannot be tense and relaxed at the same time. By learning to relax one reduces tension. In the same way, when one grows in certain areas some negative and harmful attitudes no longer have a place. Some problems may be dealt with better simply because a person has gained new strength. Some interpersonal concerns are resolved because a person has a new awareness. In this sense real healing (which is what the word "therapy" actually means) takes place. But the focus is not on problems; it is on growth.

Spiritual growth groups are valuable in many ways. We all need growth. No one ever attains full potential—that is one of the exciting things about life. It is like golf. No one ever gets so good he can't take a few strokes off his score. The potential of the mind and spirit is unlimited.

Such a group provides opportunities for sharing and belonging. There is the story of the little boy who went in to his mother and said, "Mommy, I wish I was two little puppies so I could play together." He was expressing a basic human need, one that is often denied people in our mechanized, streamlined, materialistic, impersonal culture. If a spiritual growth group did nothing more than provide an opportunity for belonging to a like-minded group of caring, seeking persons it would be worthwhile.

Then there is the educational value mentioned earlier. Perhaps a better term is "learning": the learning that takes place from the contribution of a leader, the learning that takes place in listening to others as they evaluate the same thoughts and ideas that we are concerned with. There is the learning, commonly referred to as "insight," which comes when we verbalize and clarify our own thoughts and feelings. And in this particular case there is the learning that comes as one discusses the deep thoughts and feelings that great men and women of faith through the centuries have expressed in their prayers.

In addition to its value for the individual, a growth group fulfills a need for the church as well. Churches need small groups to create a spirit of fellowship, to provide opportunities for friendship and understanding. This is especially true in larger churches where many people may worship together but not know each other as persons.

The next chapter suggests how some of these ideas can be put into practice.

PLANNING AND CONDUCTING A SPIRITUAL GROWTH GROUP

A spiritual growth group such as we are proposing here is based on three basic assumptions or presuppositions:

1. In the prayers of the religious leaders (past and present) we have a primary source for an understanding of the religious life.

2. People have the capacity to deepen their understanding and to grow. Most people have a potential far beyond what they have realized.

3. This capacity for growth is enriched, guided, and deepened when it is shared with others with similar purposes and desires.

What are some of the practical considerations that need to be taken into account in planning and conducting such a group? What principles and procedures should guide its operation?

Materials

Someone must select the prayers that are to be discussed. In most cases the leader does this, although there is some value in letting the group share in the search and selection of material to be discussed.

One group in which the leader was providing the material asked if they could take turns in selecting material. The members of the group each chose prayers for one meeting, and told why they had made their individual selections. This seemed to add a new dimension to the discussion. It not only divided the responsibility which almost always adds to the personal involvement, but personalized it as individuals told why particular prayers had unique meaning to them.

A major section of this manual includes prayers that could be used for discussion, together with introductory and interpretative statements about them and their authors. Another chapter describes general sources. An appendix lists books of prayers.

We feel that the prayers should be drawn from a variety of sources. They should represent many personalities, many denominations, many nationalities, many cultures, and many periods in history. They could conceivably all be drawn from one author or one period, but this would put some limits on the experience.

The prayers should be selected and used as an expression of man's spiritual quest, as a record of man's striving. This is not an argument for or against prayer; there may be a place for such a discussion, but that is not the purpose here. These are selected as examples of others' thoughts which can be a guide and a stimulus to our own.

In almost all such expressions we find very honest statements. As Dean Sperry has said, we have to be honest and sincere in prayer. We find that these people who recorded their honest and sincere feelings in prayer shared all the frustrations, doubts, anxieties, and feelings of guilt that we have known. This in itself is somewhat reassuring. It helps to know that the giants of the faith knew these experiences also. What we have in their prayers is intimations of their struggles, their doubts, anxieties, and guilt. We also have a testimony and a witness to their faith. We find evidences of their joy, courage, their confidence and trust. The purpose of the discussion is to attempt to understand both their struggle and their triumph, how one led to the other, and how this applies to us.

Logistics

Some practical matters need to be settled. Where does the group meet? How often and for how long? The place should be one that is convenient to most members of the group, one that is relatively free from distractions and interruptions such as phone calls or other people coming and going. It should be provided with chairs that are comfortable, but not too comfortable.

Some prefer a church because it is usually free from distractions and the building itself has a symbolic meaning. It stands for and is dedicated to spiritual truths and values. Much can also be said for the symbolic value of a home. Each group can decide such matters for itself. Wherever a group meets, church, home, or elsewhere, if possible it should be in a setting where people can be seated facing one another. A group *can* meet in a classroom setting with rows of straight chairs facing the front, or in a sanctuary or chapel with pews, but this is a disadvantage.

The time for the starting and closing of the meeting should be clearly understood. Both should be honored. This is important. The members of the group commit themselves to being present, on time, and staying through. The length of the meeting should also be determined by the group. We feel that an hour is the minimum if one is to attain maximum value, and beyond two hours elements such as fatigue set in and can produce negative feelings.

It is also good to have a termination date set in advance. A group can decide to continue after this if they wish. It is far better for a group to come to a termination date and want to continue than to feel they would like to discontinue and not know how. We have seen groups which met for single sessions only and have proved to be of real value, but for the most effectiveness we feel that six to eight sessions is about right.

The size of the group should be kept relatively small. We would say from six to twelve people. A group any smaller than this does not allow for enough variety of opinion and may develop too intense an involvement. A group beyond twelve or fifteen does not allow for enough interaction. When a group becomes larger than that, it should be divided into smaller groups. As Clinebell says, the group should be "small enough to share and care."

One variation which we have used is to have a larger group meet for an introduction of the prayers, then divide into smaller groups for the discussion.

It is usually felt best to meet once a week, although a group can meet every other week without any great loss of effectiveness. Any longer time lapse does reduce the value.

Leadership

There are a whole variety of approaches to leadership that can be used. There are also some that should not be used. The "leader dominant" approach, where the leader assumes the role of teacher and informs the group, does not fit. That is valuable for some purposes, but not here.

If a group has a leader who accepts the responsibility for organizing the group, preparing the materials, and leading the discussion, that is fine. He should be very much a part of the group, however, sharing his own reactions to the material but not in an authoritarian manner.

Some prefer co-leaders. Two people share the responsibility for providing material, etc. One very helpful way, if it could be arranged, would be for one leader, with theological training, to represent the religious field, and the other, with psychological training, to represent the mental health field.

Groups can be conducted very effectively without any leaders. In this approach the group takes turns in preparing the materials and leading the discussion. A very common procedure would be for the pastor (or some other leader) to provide leadership for the first two or three sessions and then let the group take over and proceed on its own. It is not uncommon for the discussion to improve when the group assumes responsibility for its own leadership. We do not need to discuss the principles and rules of group leadership here; it has been done many times. A bibliography of publications on the subject is included in the Appendix.

Procedures

One of the beauties of the spiritual growth group is that it is so simple. The meeting may open with a devotional period of silence, a passage of Scripture, or prayer, as the group prefers. It may simply start by reading the prayers to be discussed. This in itself is a devotional experience.

Three prayers are distributed to the group for discussion. It is important that they be duplicated and placed in each person's hand. Very seldom are all three discussed. The value of having several is that it provides a fairly wide range of possibilities for discussion. Sometimes the discussion will settle on just one prayer or even one phrase of a prayer. It is not uncommon for a group to become so involved in the discussion of an idea presented that they will want to continue it at another session.

There may be occasions when a more lengthy prayer is used, and then only one will be presented. We know of a group that used one of Fosdick's pastoral prayers as a basis of discussion. In our judgment Fosdick's prayers are among the most valuable of all the literature available in this field, but each one takes up two full pages of print, and very large pages at that. Each prayer has at least five or six major themes and there is ample material for discussion. On the nights when a group uses prayers of this length, they would obviously not use three.

After the prayers have been distributed, a brief background of the author's life will be given when the author is known, or anything else that is pertinent to an understanding of the prayer, such as the time or place in which it was written. Some examples of how this can be done are included in the next section.

The prayers are then read aloud. Some prefer to read them twice. The discussion that follows will be determined entirely by the group reactions to the content of the prayers. Any ideas, feelings, or thoughts that are suggested are appropriate. As anyone familiar with groups would expect, very often the discussion moves from the feelings and thoughts of the author to the feelings or experiences of persons in the group—which, of course, is the purpose of the whole procedure.

Although the most value will be derived from the experience if all members participate in the discussion, no one need feel embarrassed or feel that he or she has to speak if he or she prefers to sit quietly and listen. There are some kinds of groups where individuals must be confronted and required to speak or show their feelings. We doubt if that is necessary or even desirable here. In most cases everyone is drawn into the discussion sooner or later.

Covenant

Some groups speak of a contract or an agreement they require of all persons desiring to participate in the experience. We prefer the word "covenant." "Covenant" is a biblical term that means a "solemn agreement." Since the success of a spiritual growth group depends primarily on the sincerity and commitment of those who participate, a contract or covenant is very valuable. Some simply state it and either get or assume agreement. It is more effective if it is prepared and duplicated and people sign the covenant agreement.

Two approaches can be used in the preparation of a covenant. A leader can prepare a covenant and ask people to agree to it, or a group can prepare their own covenant and then make their commitment.

The content of the covenant should include whatever the leader or the group feels is pertinent to the goals of the group. Most such statements include such matters as attendance and participation mentioned above. For example, most groups ask members to agree to attend all sessions unless circumstances make it impossible to do so.

If groups share leadership this is included in the covenant. If expenses are involved this also is a matter that should be mentioned.

Since some discussions may become fairly personal, and since on occasion, owing to the atmosphere of the group, one may say things or reveal things about oneself one did not anticipate doing, it is advisable to include in the covenant a pledge of confidentiality. Although these are not therapy groups, a person has the same right here as in a therapy group, and that is to feel that if he or she does discuss personal matters they will not be repeated or discussed outside the group.

Some groups include a covenant to pray for the group each day. This may take only three or four minutes, but it would continue for the duration of the sessions. Such a prayer should be for both the group, the individual members of it, and oneself. It should be a prayer that expresses a sincere concern about the group. It should be a prayer that growth will take place, that understanding will be deepened, that an awareness of the power of the Spirit will become increasingly real.

Some Possible Problems

We believe these procedures will work, but there is nothing magical about them. A spiritual growth group is subject to the same problems that arise in any other group. Some people talk too much and arouse resistance in others. Some may become bored and want to drop out. Some troubled persons may find their way into the group. In fact, troubled persons are looking for all sorts of solutions and may seek out the group. They may need referral for counseling or psychotherapy, for we do not mean to imply that the group takes the place of individual counseling or therapy. Some people may have higher expectations than the group can fulfill and expect sudden transformation and change. We think change is possible, but by its very definition growth is slow: "first the blade, then the ear, then the full grain in the ear" (Mark 4:28 RSV).

Two dangers that need to be avoided are cliquishness and self-righteousness. What the church does not need is cliques. There is a tendency for some groups to develop a self-righteousness, an in-group—out-group feeling. This needs to be avoided. Self-righteousness and spiritual growth are opposites.

Although most groups confine their emphases to the growth experience described here, such a program as this can also be combined with other emphases. It could follow a Bible study period, or could be part of a service project, for example.

SOURCES FOR A STUDY OF PRAYERS

Anyone wanting to make a personal study of prayers has a wide selection of materials to choose from. The prayers may be selected for one's personal understanding and growth or materials for a growth group as described in this manual.

Scripture

For prayers, as always, the Bible is a primary source. In the narrative books of the Old Testament early heroes such as Gideon and David were pictured as men of prayer. The prophets like Jeremiah and Isaiah also took both their complaints and their praise to God.

The book of Psalms is the richest source, for every expression of prayer is found in its pages.

The Twenty-fifth Psalm begins with a prayer of confidence and trust:

> To thee, O Lord, I lift up my soul.
> O my God, in thee I trust. (Psalm 25:1 RSV)

Sometimes the prayers are filled with questions and uncertainty:

> Why dost thou stand afar off, O Lord?
> Why dost thou hide thyself in times of trouble?
> (Psalm 10:1 RSV)

There are many prayers of confession:

> Wash me thoroughly from my iniquity,
>   and cleanse me from my sin! (Psalm 51:2 RSV)

Sometimes there are prayers of petition and aspiration:

Let the words of my mouth and the meditation
     of my heart
   be acceptable in thy sight,
   O Lord, my rock and my redeemer.
                              (Psalm 19:14 RSV)

Over and over there are prayers of gratitude:

     We give thanks to thee, O God;
        we give thanks;
     we call on thy name and recount
        thy wondrous deeds. (Psalm 75:1 RSV)

Here is a veritable storehouse of prayers, which covers the whole range of prayer and religious experience.

In the New Testament Jesus is pictured as a man of prayer. At the beginning of each day, at the close of each day, he went apart to pray. Each coming crisis he faced first in prayer. Some of these prayers are recorded in the Gospels. Of course, the one that is most familiar is the model prayer which is found in two places in slightly varied form. In Luke it comes as a response to the disciples' request "Lord, teach us to pray" (11:1 RSV). In Matthew 6:7-14 it is included in the Sermon on the Mount in the section where Jesus is discussing religious activities such as the giving of alms, prayer, and fasting. In the Pauline and other epistles in the New Testament the authors are revealed as men of prayer. The benedictions which conclude most of the letters are rich in theological content and practical religious value. (See especially Romans 16:25-27; 2 Corinthians 13:14.)

A study of Paul's benedictions alone could be worthwhile. But the most familiar of all benedictions is that of the little Letter of Jude: "Now to him who is able to keep you from falling and to present you without blemish before the presence of his glory with rejoicing, to the only God, our Savior through Jesus Christ our Lord, be glory, majesty, dominion, and authority, before all time and now and for ever" (vv. 24-25 RSV).

The Devotional Classics

A classic is defined as "a work of enduring excellence." Some say no literary work can be considered a classic until it has survived three hundred years. There are some outstanding classics of the devotional life that are works of such excellence that they have survived for centuries. They continue to be republished generation after generation because they speak to a universal need that is common to all—the need to feel a relationship with God.

Brother Lawrence's *Practice of the Presence of God*, written in the seventeenth century, is helpful because it creates a mood of prayer. Brother Lawrence was no scholar and had no eminence; but his devotional life was so real and so profound that others sought his secret. His little book consists of a series of conversations and some letters in which he explains that one simply learns to "practice the presence of God" in all one's daily tasks.

Others of the classics include prayers which give us an insight into the religious thought and the nature of the prayer life of the saints. Such a work is Thomas a Kempis' *Imitation of Christ*, of which it is said, it has gone through more reprintings than any book except the Bible. It was written first in the fifteenth century as a devotional guide for novices in the monastery. Augustine's *Confessions* also includes many examples of profound meaningful prayer.

Such prayers are expressed in the terminology and the thought forms of their day, but they contain much that is common to the hopes and striving, the perplexities and concerns, of every generation.

For a history of the devotional classics and a psychological evaluation of their meaning see E. Glenn Hinson and Wayne E. Oates, *Seekers After Mature Faith* (Word Books, 1968).

Contemporary Publications

Many contemporary authors have published books of prayers. These have not yet survived the required three hundred years, so they cannot be listed as classics in that sense; but they have provided a source of guidance and help to many. In fact, some prefer them to the classical expressions, for they speak more in the language of today.

Georgia Harkness, who has the distinction of being the first woman theologian (in the professional sense) in America, has published many widely read theological books. She has also published several devotional guides. *Be Still and Know* (1953) is one we shall refer to again later. *Through Christ Our Lord* (Abingdon-Cokesbury Press, 1950) is based on the teachings and events in the life of Jesus.

John Baillie, a noted theologian from Edinburgh, wrote a little book whose many reprintings indicate that it may well become a classic. *A Diary of Private Prayer* is a series of thirty prayers designed to be read over a month's time, and then repeated as often as one wishes. Each prayer is printed on a separate page, while the opposite page is left blank for the reader's own thoughts or prayers. A unique feature of these meaningful prayers is that Baillie frequently leaves blanks for the reader/worshiper to fill in. If, for example, he has a prayer of confession, he will leave a series of blanks where the reader can list his or her own specific sins for which forgiveness is requested. If it is a prayer of thanksgiving or intercession, the same procedure is followed.

There are many other possible choices. If one wants to study prayers that are not old enough to be classics but are too old to be contemporary, there are the public prayers of Henry Ward Beecher, *A Book of Prayer* (1892), and, of course, Walter Rauschenbusch's *Prayers of the Social Awakening*. Rauschenbusch is recognized as the founder of the Social Gospel movement in America. He was deeply involved in the struggle for social justice at a time when to do so meant not only public criticism but hostile condemnation. He was also a man of profound religious faith and a deep devotional spirit. He combined both his social concern and his devotional spirit in these prayers.

Many of them grew out of life situations. He said he would ride on railroad trains, and wherever he went he would meditate on the problems of the people he saw. He said, "I then would shut out of my mind everything else but the needs of these people." He felt his prayers were the fruits of these meditations.

One simple example is the prayer "In Remembrance of Daily Food and Those Who Produce and Gather It":

Our Father, Thou art the final source of all our comforts and to Thee we render thanks for this food. But we also remember in gratitude the many men and women whose labor was necessary to produce it, and who gathered it from the land and afar from the sea for our sustenance. Grant that they too may enjoy the fruit of their labor without want, and may be bound up with us in a fellowship of thankful hearts.

More recently there have appeared such books as Walter Russell Bowie's *Lift Up Your Hearts* or William Barclay's *A Guide to Daily Prayer*. Barclay uses very contemporary and earthy phrases, such as—

O God, you are a God of peace, and I am a worrier. Take away my worry and give me some of your peace. (P. 88)

Help me to meet people courteously, and, if need be, to suffer fools gladly. (P. 20)

Help me always to speak a word of praise, whenever a word of praise is possible—and sometimes even when it is not possible. (P. 66)

O God, give me tonight a heart content and a mind at rest, so that I may sleep in peace and rise in strength. (P. 57)

If one wants even more contemporary language, the language of youth, the language of the "now generation," one will find value in Malcolm Boyd's *Are You Running with Me, Jesus?*

The prayer which gives the book its title is illustrative of what we find here:

I've got to move fast ... get into the bathroom, wash up, grab a bite to eat, and run some more.

I just don't feel like it, Lord. What I really want to do is to get back into bed, pull up the covers, and sleep. All I seem to want today is the big sleep, and here I've got to run all over again.

Where am I running? You know these things I can't understand. It's not that I need to have you tell me. What counts most is just that somebody knows, and it's you. That helps a lot.

So I'll follow along, okay? But lead, Lord. Now I've got to run. Are you running with me, Jesus? (P. 19)

All serious students of prayers should study Harry Emerson Fosdick's *Book of Public Prayers* (1959). These are classics of pastoral prayers prepared for public worship, but they can serve equally well as the basis for private meditation or group discussion.

Other places where prayers are occasionally found are in books of sermons, where a prayer accompanies a sermon, and in biographies and autobiographies. Prayers in autobiographies are much more rare, but when they do appear they are usually related to a meaningful incident in a person's life, such as Bushnell's prayer for faith in a time of great uncertainty and confusion (pp. 87-88), or Luther's prayer for courage when he was on trial before the Diet of Worms (p. 85).

The Hymnbook

One should not overlook the hymnbook in the quest for suitable prayers. Many of the best-loved hymns were first written as prayers and then later were set to music and found their way into the hymnbook. Just as in the book of Psalms, all expressions of prayer are found in the hymnbook. Van Dyke's "Joyful, Joyful, we adore Thee" is a prayer of praise. Washington Gladden's "O Master, Let Me Walk with Thee" is a prayer of petition, a request for the privilege of sharing in a life of service. "Take My Life, and Let It Be Consecrated, Lord, to Thee" is a prayer of commitment. "Spirit of God, Descend upon My Heart" is what Fosdick would call a prayer of receptivity, a form of prayer too often neglected.

Anthologies and Collections

There are some very useful anthologies and collections which have brought together some of the finest expressions of prayer both past and present and made them available in one publication. *The Student Prayerbook*, edited by a committee under the chairmanship of John Oliver Nelson (Association Press, 1953), is one such volume. *Prayers for Services*, edited by Morgan Phelps Noyes, is another.

Some mention should be made at this point of Fosdick's *The Meaning of Prayer*. It is much more than an anthology, but the many prayers that are included fulfill the same purpose as an anthology. It first appeared in 1915 as a devotional guide for college students. Since then it has gone through repeated printings and, like Baillie's book, can rightfully be called a contemporary classic.

It includes both a discussion about prayer and a collection of prayers. It is designed so it can be read daily, with a thought, a text, and prayer for each day of the week for ten weeks. The prayers that are used were selected from a wide variety of sources and comprise an anthology in themselves. They have further value in that they are related to some theme or idea about prayer and are thus illustrative of what prayer can be.

An interesting background to this book was provided by Dr. Fosdick himself in a sermon late in his career. He said he had once experienced a time of doubt and uncertainty that was very intense. When, later, people asked him why as a young man he wrote a book on prayer, he replied that that book came out of young manhood's struggle. He said there was a time when he desperately needed something to hang on to and the book about prayer was the result.

This was followed by two other publications following the same format: *The Meaning of Faith* (1917) and *The Meaning of Service* (1920).

Anyone who is serious about deepening his religious knowledge and spiritual growth may want to make his own anthology. He should search the available material, past and present, and select those prayers that "speak to his condition" to have on hand for continued study and meditation.

THE DEVELOPMENT OF
SPIRITUAL GROWTH
BETWEEN SESSIONS

One of the limitations of traditional counseling and psychotherapy is that they confine their activities to the counseling hour and make little use of the time between sessions. But the motivation that brought people to counseling can also be directed toward meaningful tasks at other times. The same principle applies to a growth group: the motivation that causes one to attend a growth group can be used to foster growth between sessions.

Some people do not know what such activities are, and the group performs a useful function if it makes them aware of the possibilities. There is also the added incentive that comes if one is aware that others are following similar procedures. This is extended a step further if they share experiences and make them the basis of the discussion or feed them into the group discussions. If a group agrees that activities between sessions are important, they can be written into the covenant, but we prefer that they be voluntary. The following are suggestions only. Other projects could be added, and some people might not want to include some of the ones listed here.

Bible Study. This could be a reading of the biblical teachings on prayer, or it could be the reading of a single book or section. The book of Psalms is ideal since so many of its chapters are prayers.

General Reading. The group could agree to read together a book related to the overall purpose of the group. This could be a book on prayer such as Fosdick's *The Meaning of Prayer*, or Magee's *Reality and Prayer.* It could be a book on groups, such as Reid's *Groups Alive–Church Alive*, or one on communication, such as Reuel Howe's *Miracle of Dialogue.*

Meditation and Prayer. The prayers used in the group could be used as a basis for meditation. This is discussed more fully in the next section, "The Use of Prayers as a Guide to Prayer and Meditation."

Relaxation Training. Meditation is enhanced if one can cultivate the art of relaxation. This is valuable in itself because it greatly reduces tension, for you can't be tense and relaxed at the same time. Relaxation can be learned. Some of the methods that have been proved useful are described in the appendix on relaxation training. Fifteen minutes a day in complete relaxation can have definite benefits.

Writing Out One's Own Prayers. There is a real value in writing out one's prayers. Just the discipline of thinking them through is helpful. There is something about putting things down on paper that clarifies and reinforces ideas. There is a value in just writing out one's thoughts. It reduces tension. It often leads to insight. One reason some of the saints and spiritual leaders of the past had such insight may have been that they kept personal diaries: spiritual autobiographical statements in which they recorded their thoughts and sometimes wrote out their prayers. (See the appendix on free writing for further discussion of the value of writing.)

Intercessory Prayer. In discussing covenants we mentioned that many groups agree to pray for the group. This should be done regularly throughout the experience. Such discipline in intercession can be a real experience of spiritual growth and commitment.

Furthermore experience testifies that it does produce results.

You may think of other activities the group could share, either individually or as a group. The time between sessions may prove to be as valuable as the time the group spends together.

THE USE OF PRAYERS AS A GUIDE TO INDIVIDUAL PRAYER AND MEDITATION

The experience of the group can carry over and be a stimulus that will motivate and enrich one's personal religious life. It may also provide some resources that can be useful. Most people could use some help in deepening and enriching their own private religious lives.

Studying and meditating upon the prayers of others is one resource that is seldom utilized but which has great value. In other areas, from art to athletics, if we want to understand a field we study the masters. We turn for guidance to those who do it best, we look to the authorities, we have confidence in those whose experience is extensive. Why not do the same with prayer?

This is not a suggestion that the prayers of others can or should take the place of our own. It is a statement of faith. Harry Emerson Fosdick, who spoke so frequently of prayer, said, "As one reads the great prayers of the church he sees that in this realm supremely the people of God have prayed with confidence, have expected answer and have not been disappointed" (*The Meaning of Prayer*, p. 111). Prayer has been a real force in the lives of others; it can be in ours. In studying and pondering their prayers we have one of the best resources for learning how to grow spiritually.

Study of the prayers of others is valuable in many ways. It is educational, for one thing. A knowledge of how they have prayed tells us a great deal about the inner lives and thoughts of the great men and women of faith, both past and present. It gives us an insight into the thoughts, beliefs, faith, and ideas that guided them and made them strong.

Studying great prayers teaches us how to pray. We all need models in all areas of life. A study of prayers guides us, at times challenges us, and awakens within us new ideas about the content of prayer.

There is a tendency in many people's lives to confine prayers to petition and to neglect some of the other expressions that should be a part of everyone's spiritual experience, such as adoration, praise, confession, communion, dedication, commitment. There is also a tendency to be repetitious and monotonous in our expressions of prayer. Studying the prayers of men and women of faith broadens the scope and enriches the possibilities of prayer.

Studying prayers also creates the mood of prayer. This may be one of its greatest values. Our lives are filled with so many activities; the secular impact of our society, the demands upon our time, energy, and attention, are so great that it is at times difficult to get into a mood of prayer. A few minutes of quiet meditation on the prayers of others can help us do so.

Studying the prayers of others not only provides a model but can be a means through which great expressions of prayer become our own prayers. Some resist this, saying that no one else can offer our prayers for us. Yet this method has been used for centuries. It was the custom of the ancient rabbis to give their followers prayers to learn. These prayers included the ideas they thought were important and should be included in prayer. Jesus used the same method with his disciples when he taught them the Lord's Prayer. He gave them a model which he said should become their own. It is only possible when we so familiarize ourselves with others, so identify ourselves with them, that their thoughts become our thoughts, their prayers become our prayers.

Now for some practical suggestions as to how this can be done. Make use of the prayers that are discussed in the group. After you have had the benefit of the group's reaction to them they can become the basis for your own personal meditation. Read and study as widely as possible in the literature that includes prayers. A great variety of material is available. What appeals to one may not appeal to another. Some prefer the prayers of the saints; some prefer more contemporary expressions. Some prefer the stately language of the prayerbook, some the contemporary language of modern man. It does not matter which you choose; find what creates the spirit and mood in you.

Create your own anthology. Start a file or keep a notebook of those prayers that speak to you personally. After you have made your selection return to them repeatedly. Reading prayers is like reading poetry or Scripture. You get a different meaning with each reading. As your experience grows, so does your understanding. Read appreciatively. This does not mean one shuts off one's critical faculties. It does not mean one necessarily agrees with all the theological ideas that are expressed. It does mean one reads prayers in a different frame of mind from that in which one reads a novel, a textbook, or the newspaper. Read meditatively, in a relaxed state of mind and body. Cultivate the capacity to relax, then while relaxed read, ponder, meditate. Let the mind go where it will, then maybe read the prayer again, and again. Finally, and most important, pray. Pray spontaneously, pray trustfully, use words and phrases from the prayers, if they seem natural to you —but pray. Study, read, ponder, meditate, memorize; let the authors' spirits speak to your spirit, and then pray.

WHAT OTHERS HAVE DONE

In this chapter we shall discuss some of the experiences of those who have led spiritual growth groups as well as those who have participated in them.

Our first attempt at using this procedure was with a group of clergymen. Some were advanced theological students. Some were full-time parish pastors. The prayer that was used was the one found on page 62 in the section on selected prayers.

It contains the sentence "We bring our work to be

sanctified, our wounds to be healed, our sins to be forgiven, our hopes to be renewed."

We thought this might be a statement that would have meaning for clergymen and anticipated a discussion on "we bring our work to be sanctified." Many clergymen are having difficulty with their vocational identity. Some question their calling. In fact, we knew that some of this group were facing such problems. We expected a discussion of vocation and calling.

Instead they picked up on another phrase in the prayer, "Take us out of the loneliness of self, and fill us with the fullness of Thy truth and love." They centered their thought on the word "loneliness." They spoke of the widespread loneliness that exists today. They spoke with real understanding of the fact that we live in a culture that depersonalizes, isolates, and in many ways accentuates the problem of loneliness. They discussed the number of lonely people they have in their congregations and shared their thinking on how that loneliness can be helped.

This went on for some time, and then one member of the group spoke up and said, "We're dodging the issue. We're lonely. The ministry is a lonely profession. My wife is lonely in the parsonage." What followed then was a most worthwhile period of sharing and support.

It occurred to us afterward that here was a problem that many, if not all, in the group faced, and one that might never have been discussed and shared except for a phrase in a prayer that made it quite natural to do so.

A group of laymen were discussing a prayer by Martin Luther. They spoke of how honest Luther was with God. This led to an examination of their own integrity and honesty—both with God and with each other. Some shared personal experiences. The leader of the group said, "In sharing of these instances, I could feel the level of trust really deepen and feel people really being supportive and concerned for the persons who were witnessing." This is another instance of a need that would have remained unexamined and unexpressed except for the fact that a prayer first uttered over four hundred years ago brought it forth.

There was one member of the first group, a young associate pastor in a suburban church, who was impressed by the experience and utilized it in his church. We asked him to write up a statement of what developed. The following account is a summary of their experience.

In the pastor's words: "The first meeting of this group occurred in the parlor of the church at 7:30 P.M. on a Thursday evening. Because we are meeting on Thursday after a day's work, we wear informal attire and also provide a nursery for the children. The members move freely about, if necessary, during the meeting, and refreshments are provided which add to the air of informality.

"The room itself is ideal for small-group interaction. The chairs are extremely comfortable, the room soundproof. Well-chosen pictures, objects and carpeting aid in making the atmosphere relaxed and enjoyable."

The group consisted of five young couples: a neurologist and his wife, who is a vocational guidance counselor; an electrical engineer and his wife, who works in a small shop; a carpenter and his wife, who works in a bank; an engineer and his wife, who is a teacher; a minister (who we presume was also the leader of the group) and his wife, who is a teacher.

The meeting opened with a prayer. Then the leader made a brief statement about prayer in general and asked for the group's reactions to prayer. Their responses reveal their diverse attitudes toward prayer as such.

They ranged from "It has been extremely important for me to pray, not necessarily with words because I feel God knows all about me and my needs" to "Prayer means nothing to me. I cannot conceive that the God who created this infinite universe would be able to hear a small voice directed towards him."

One couple said, "We are waiting to learn more about prayer before we can offer any reaction. However, both of us want to believe that it holds great power." Another person said he "didn't try hard enough to know."

The leader summarized the brief discussion, pointing out that they did have different viewpoints, owing to different backgrounds, and introduced the idea of discussing prayers themselves rather than ideas about prayer.

He read the prayer by Robert Louis Stevenson which begins, "The day returns and brings us the petty round of irritating concerns and duties" (p. 58). As he describes it: "I read the prayer without emphasis to avoid fixing their attention on any one point. I then asked for reactions. The first one was criticizing the rotten way I read it." Other reactions were: "That really hits home with me—my days are usually so busy that by the time I'm ready to go to bed my eyes are glued open," and "I don't know why, but that's good," and "Say, that's like you're talking to someone. I can't stand it when prayers are divided into Part A, Part B, and Part C." A very fruitful discussion followed.

A young pastor in a suburban church has been using this plan for a period of five months. We asked him to provide us with a report of some of his group's experiences. He prepared a tape which outlined their procedures, including some of the problems they experienced and some of the valuable results.

They initiated the program with a general announcement that a prayer fellowship would be held and everyone was welcome. The term itself created some hesitation. People feared they would be asked to pray aloud and refused to come. When they became aware of the nature of the program, some of these same people came and participated freely; in fact, several came who had not participated in any other activities of the church other than morning worship.

The group that attended ranged from ten to twenty-five or twenty-six. When there were more than twelve, they divided up into pairs. They used this pairing off first as a means of getting to know one another on a deeper level than simply saying "hi" on Sunday morning.

The pastor said, "We found this to be one of the real benefits of the prayer fellowship ... a deepening and intensifying experience of fellowship —koinonia—in which persons are beginning to share on a trusting and feeling level with other

Christians." While they were encouraged to share, they were not pushed to go beyond anything they felt comfortable doing. While some found even this to be difficult, many testified to the "feeling of closeness, warmth and support that comes from sharing with one another."

The pastor listed this as the first benefit they had received from the groups. The second was "the experience of learning." He said, "In the process of our discussion of these various issues that are related to prayer we bring in ideas of our own. I can remember the discussion, quite a lengthy discussion in fact, on confession. We discussed confession in the context of Christian faith and the role of guilt and how guilt is removed from a Christian standpoint. We got into issues of salvation, how a person is saved, why confession is necessary, why guilt plagues our lives and paralyzes and restricts us. The discussion was meaningful and fruitful and really became a learning experience because we went to our Bibles and looked at passages on confession and guilt and examined them in order to be able to answer questions that had arisen during the course of our discussion."

The final value that he listed was "witness": "When persons express their faith in an unstructured give-and-take level which seems to have a high degree of trust, we all seem to benefit from the witness of faith that is offered."

He described the whole experience as "an open, dynamic type of experience in which, I believe, using Keith Miller's phrase, people can come and for a few moments when they feel the need in their lives they can 'taste of new wine' and go away renewed and refreshed. I have felt very much the power of

God's Spirit and presence in the midst of our fellowship. I must confess that at the beginning of our first session, I tried to do too much to program in a spiritual feeling ... but it wasn't needed, because the reality of God's presence, the power that prayer has in and of itself, was there regardless of the devices one tries to use to invoke the Spirit. And the real power that seems to be in our praying together is the supporting, trusting relationship, the deepening of love and the experience in the sharing together, in the witnessing together, and in the praying together that we have. The prayer fellowship has become a very vital part of our church. It is not making a lot of ripples, it is not dramatically transforming the church overnight; it is simply helping people grow and mature and share as Christians."

Some people who have participated in such groups have been asked to evaluate their experience, to state what it meant to them. The following statements are expressions of people from different groups:

"This is the first time that I have ever been involved in such a group and I learned a lot about myself and other people. Using the prayers, or what have you, as a springboard to start the discussion sure does help. This gave everyone a common foothold to grab onto. I was afraid that I would miss the last group session because I am leaving to go home the day before. But luckily it has been moved up and I don't have to miss it at all."

"The group has helped us to feel closer to each other and to the church. It has really helped us to understand each other. We have shared our joys and our sorrows, learning how to pray and for what we should pray. Our faith has been strengthened."

"I have appreciated friendliness and feelings of love toward me—I hope to extend my feelings in the same way and to lose some of my shyness."

"It [the group] helps us to know each other better, and share our problems as well as our joys .... We all need to share our concern and love for each other, and this is one way to do this, as we are able to discuss things one might not know about otherwise."

An advanced seminary student who had participated in several different groups both in and out of the church spoke rather critically of some church growth groups because they seemed to "struggle" to be religious. He felt the use of prayers as a starting point resolved that problem. "Beginning with devotional material opens the group to a depth of experience more rapidly than any group I have participated in before. That group which met only briefly was one of the most meaningful experiences of my seminary experience. The members of that group still feel very close and free with one another.

"This group idea begins with religious subject matter and one does not feel manipulated into a therapy group in the name of faith.

"The availability of material makes the variety of subject matter sufficient to reach the needs and feelings of any group."

Another seminary student who participated in one of the groups admitted that his own devotional life had dropped considerably while in seminary. This is a not uncommon experience. As Dr. Wieman pointed out some time ago, it is difficult to study religion and be religious at the same time. Or as the student put it, "After viewing Christianity from the analytical side all day, I lost touch with the personal life of devotion and meditation."

He described his experience in the group this way: "In small groups we could explore areas as our interest dictated. For the first time, I could actually bring out problems that I was having myself, and the group often provided help. I'm not talking about practical church problems, but personal problems that often grew out of church relationships. I found out that others often feel like I do, but don't know where to turn for help."

Not all experiences will be positive. After a prayer had been read one person replied, "That's a lot of _____." Another person, a young man, after a prayer of Harry Emerson Fosdick's had been read said it made him angry. The prayer was so well phrased, so perfectly expressed, he said, he couldn't measure up and that made him mad. A rather frequent remark, especially about the more classical prayers, is that the language is too flowery. "I don't feel comfortable with 'Thees' and 'Thous.'"

One group used the prayer of Bishop Leofric written in the eleventh century (p. 83). The reaction was quite negative. They said it was too stiff and formal. The leader read it again, changing "Thy" and "Thou" to your and you, etc. This helped a little, but the response was still negative. The leader, showing considerable persistence, then asked them to meditate on each phrase, to attempt to recover the author's feeling. This helped, he said, but it never did develop the response he received from other prayers.

Another group was discussing a prayer of

gratitude and praise. Anticipating a discussion that would point out the many things for which we should be grateful, the group was surprised when a woman said, "I have nothing to thank God for."

One woman expressed how she had both positive and negative feelings in the group. In fact, her statement is an example of how one can use the group experience and the content of the prayers to work through negative feelings to a positive healthy expression: "it ... has been an emotional experience in a way I did not expect. I expected to come and find personal strength to face my problems. Instead, sometimes I go away shaken because I have had to voice my pains, and my sadness if I was to be honest in my participation. Other times when this was not the pattern ... when it centered on group discussion and participation, I did receive spiritual refreshment and renewed strength and joy."

On the whole the negative responses have been small compared with the positive results. Some negative reactions are to be expected. No sermon, book, or class appeals equally to all people.

The fact that some negative reactions occur points up the necessity of having several selections available for each session. If one prayer does not stimulate discussion, move to one that does, rather than belabor the issue.

Negative reactions aren't all without value. A person's critical or negative responses may alert the leader or pastor to that person's need of which he was unaware. This may be followed up with a call or a discussion outside the group.

It has also been our experience that some negative responses soon turned to positive ones with a bit of patience and understanding by the group and the leader.

All in all the experiences thus far indicate that this procedure can lead to both group understanding and individual insight and religious growth. We urge others to try this method, experiment with it, modify it if they wish, but to use it to help people attain spiritual growth and maturity. We would appreciate hearing of any interesting experiences, and of modifications or improvements anyone has made.

II
COMMENTARIES
ON SELECTED
PRAYERS

The following pages include samples of prayers that have been used as the basis of discussion, together with the kinds of introductory statements that were used to present them. Again, these are only suggestions. A group can find other prayers, or may prefer to prepare their own commentaries on them.

TEACH US TO PRAY

It is interesting to note that the only thing the disciples ever asked Jesus to teach them was how to pray. These men had prayed all their lives. When Jesus prayed it was different. Something seemed to happen. They sensed it. His very countenance was changed. They said, "Lord, teach us to pray." He responded by teaching them the Lord's Prayer.

This is a request we all need to make. No matter how long we have been used to praying, or how frequently, there are greater experiences to be attained.

In the prayer that follows, the same desire that was

voiced by the disciples is expressed again, with the recognition that it is through prayer that one grows in prayer.

Lord, teach us how to pray. Our faltering speech but faintly utters the yearnings of our hearts. Thou art the inspirer and hearer of prayer. Help us to be Thy loving and prayerful children. Give us to know the joy of fellowship with Thee, and may the Master's example of prayerfulness give us confidence to ask that we may receive. Abiding thus in communion with Thee and in loving fellowship with Christ and all our brothers, may we await with confidence the day when hope shall change to glad fruition and prayer to communion face to face. *Amen.*
—Herbert L. Willett and Charles Clayton Morrison, *The Daily Altar* (Willett, Clark & Co., 1937), p. 7

A PRAYER FOR THE DAILY TASK

Robert Louis Stevenson is one of the world's great storytellers. Everyone knows about *Treasure Island, Kidnapped, Dr. Jekyll and Mr. Hyde,* and *The Child's Garden of Verses.* Few people know he also published a book of prayers.

Not many people know, either, of his lifelong struggle with disease or the fact that most of his life he was involved in a battle with debt. There is no trace of these problems in his stories. Both *Treasure Island* and *Dr. Jekyll and Mr. Hyde* were written in bed. We think of him as a successful author, which he was, but it was not until late in his life that he got out from under the burden of debt.

He was certainly not orthodox in his religious

views, but he expressed real devotion in his prayers. In this one he talks about the daily task and some of its problems, as well as some of his hopes. It contains nothing very profound or very theological, but some of the lines are well worth pondering.

"The day returns and brings us the petty round of irritating concerns and duties." Who doesn't know what he meant? We might like glamorous activities that would all run smoothly, but life isn't that way. Most people can deal with the crises; it is the "irritating concerns and duties" that get us down.

"Help us to perform them with laughter and kind faces." Pleasantness and kindness—how much we appreciate these qualities in people we meet or live with.

"Cheerfulness and industry"—here are two qualities all too seldom combined.

Or consider the final request. "Bring us to our resting beds"—"weary," tired from honest toil, "content" (how much we need contentment or inner satisfaction), and "undishonored," with a clear conscience, free from guilt. Then one can enjoy "the gift of sleep."

It is a very commonplace prayer, simple, realistic, almost mundane; but deeply needed.

The day returns and brings us the petty round of irritating concerns and duties. Help us to perform them with laughter and kind faces; let cheerfulness abound with industry. Give us to go blithely on our business all this day, bring us to our resting beds weary and content and undishonored; and grant us in the end the gift of sleep.

–*The Works of Robert Louis Stevenson*
(Scribner's, 1898), vol. 26, p. 146

A PRAYER FOR SERENITY

We live in an age that has been described as the Age of Anxiety. It is a time of tension, worry, and strain. Everyone is aware of that. Many suggestions are being made as to how the tension can be reduced, how the strain can be alleviated. Georgia Harkness believes that one of the most effective solutions is one of the oldest—faith and prayer.

Georgia Harkness is without a doubt the most eminent woman theologian the American church has produced. She was a professor in a theological school, lectures before lay and ministerial groups, and is the author of over thirty widely read volumes. One of the constant themes of her writings has been prayer and the devotional life.

In *Prayer and the Common Life* (p. 93), she wrote: "What trust in God means in the common life is that in great matters or in small, we can keep on working, hoping, praying. To know that in God's keeping our lives are secure and in his care no good thing is ever lost is to find God's greatest boon—peace of mind and power for living."

She has expressed this thought in the following prayer. It is a prayer that is sensitive to man and his tensions and concerns, but also affirms the serenity and inner peace that comes from God.

Here we catch a reflection of the fourth chapter of the letter that Paul, who also faced tension and strain, wrote his friends at Philippi: "Have no anxiety about anything, but in everything by prayer and supplication with thanksgiving let your requests be made known to God. And the peace of God, which passes all understanding, will keep your hearts and your minds in Christ Jesus" (Philippians 4:6-7 RSV).

O God, who art the guard and guide of all who put their trust in Thee, grant us Thy peace. Thou knowest the cares that torment our spirits. Thou seest the way before us more clearly than our eyes can discern it. Forgive the anxieties that cloud our minds and consume our strength; in Thee let us rest and be strong.

Save us, O Lord, from anxious self-concern; from dark imaginings; from distrust of Thy guiding care. Give us wisdom to act and faith to wait. So shall Thy peace which passes understanding be ours. Through Jesus Christ our Lord. *Amen.*

—Georgia Harkness, *Be Still and Know* (Abingdon-Cokesbury Press, 1953), p. 11

A PRAYER OF DEDICATION AND ASPIRATION

We do not know the author of this prayer. It belongs to that large group of creations that have to be listed as "anonymous." But from its contents we do know that whoever wrote it was a keen observer of human nature and had real insights into human needs. In the second sentence he speaks of man's work, his wounds, his sins, and his hopes. He is aware of man's loneliness, his bitterness, his imperfections, but also of his visions and his hopes. Above all, he must have been a man of faith. For him God is a God of peace, "whose greatness is beyond our highest praise." It is to God that we bring our work, our wounds, our sins, our hopes, ourselves. Since

God is a God of truth and love, one can live by a basic trust in the love that is God and the good that is in ourselves.

O God of peace, we turn aside from an unquiet world, seeking rest for our spirits and light for our thoughts. We bring our work to be sanctified, our wounds to be healed, our sins to be forgiven, our hopes to be renewed, our better selves to be quickened. O Thou, in whom there is harmony, draw us to Thyself, and silence the discords of our wasteful lives. Thou who art one in all, and in whom all are one, take us out of the loneliness of self, and fill us with the fullness of Thy truth and love. Thou whose greatness is beyond our highest praise, lift us above our common littleness and our daily imperfections; send us visions of the love that is in Thee and of the good that may be in us. *Amen.*

A PRAYER OF ST. FRANCIS

St. Francis is sometimes referred to as the man who walked more closely in the footsteps of Jesus than any man in history. His story is a familiar one. Known as the playboy of Assisi, Francis led the youth of the town in all the reveling of his day; but he was unhappy. He tried making money, but that didn't satisfy. He joined himself to one of the knights, thinking, perhaps, that in conquest he could find what he sought; but he came back disillusioned.

Finally, after a long illness, he knelt in the chapel of St. Damian and prayed for guidance. The scripture of the morning was from the twenty-fifth chapter of Matthew: "For I was an hungered, and ye gave me meat: I was thirsty, and ye gave me drink ... naked, and ye clothed me." Francis felt it had been written for him.

He went out and began a career of self-forgetful service unsurpassed in Christian history. He took the coat from his own back and gave it to a beggar; he went to a leper colony to minister to the needs and suffering there. Wherever he went, he helped.

Whether or not this is an actual prayer of St. Francis no one knows, but some sources attribute it to him. It certainly expresses the spirit of St. Francis, and he in turn expressed the spirit of Christ. As much as anyone who ever lived, he gave himself, lost himself, in the interests of others.

Nothing is more needed than such a spirit in our world today. One could well say this prayer every day, meditate on it, ponder it, but above all pray it—as one's own.

> Lord, make me an instrument of Thy peace!
> Where there is hatred, let me sow love,
> Where there is injury, pardon;
> Where there is doubt, faith;
> Where there is despair, hope;
> Where there is darkness, light;
> Where there is sadness, joy.
>
> O Divine Master, grant that I may not so
>   much seek to be consoled,
> As to console;
> To be understood, as to understand;
> To be loved, as to love.
>
> For it is in giving that we receive;
> It is in pardoning that we are pardoned;
> It is in dying unto ourselves that we are
>   born to eternal life.
>
> —Attributed to St. Francis

THE REALIZATION OF GOD

Three centuries ago a Carmelite monk by the name of Brother Lawrence wrote a little book called *The Practice of the Presence of God*. It has become a devotional classic. Brother Lawrence was a simple man. He had almost no formal education. He worked in the monastery kitchen. Yet he demonstrated such obvious serenity that many people sought his counsel and guidance. He wrote a series of letters which describe his practice, and this is all he ever wrote. He didn't realize he was writing a classic. His thesis, like his life, was a simple one: the Christian life is to "practice the presence of God." This could be done anywhere. Brother Lawrence said God was just as real to him when he was in the kitchen scouring the pots and pans as when he was on his knees in the chapel.

Walter Russell Bowie lived in the twentieth century. His life was very different from Brother Lawrence's. He lived in industrialized, mechanized, streamlined, scientific America. He was highly educated. He taught in a graduate school of theology. He wrote many books. One of them was a small collection of brief prayers. His setting was very different from that of Brother Lawrence, yet he shared some of the same experiences and expressed some of the same ideas.

Though conditions have changed, the surroundings have been altered, and the environment and culture are quite different, the presence of God can be as real and is as needed in one generation as in another. This is the essence of this prayer.

O God, I bring thee this one prayer. Show me thyself. Help me to know that I am not alone, but that with me is the Friend who will not fail. Make me quick to recognize the revelations of thy presence which may come to me through what I have thought were common things; and whenever I behold thy purpose, help me to obey it, so that I may learn to know thee better and to love thee more; through Jesus Christ my Lord. *Amen.*

—Walter Russell Bowie, *Lift Up Your Hearts*, p. 23

A SCRIPTURAL PRAYER

The language of prayer is the language of Scripture. The thoughts of Scripture are a guide to prayer. The moods of Scripture are the mood of prayer. If someone will saturate himself with the words of Scripture and then through meditation, contemplation, and creative devotion appropriate these ideas and attitudes into prayer, he will find both his knowledge of Scripture and his life of prayer growing together.

In this prayer the author has taken the words of the prophet Isaiah (30:15) and the words of the psalmist (46:10) and combined them with a thought found in the Letter to the Ephesians (3:16) to create a prayer of great beauty of expression and deep spiritual insight. In this brief statement is included the biblical source of man's confidence and peace.

O God of peace, who hast taught us that in returning and rest we shall be saved, in quietness and confidence shall be our strength; by the might of thy Spirit lift us, we pray thee, to thy presence, where we may be still and know that thou art God, through Jesus Christ our Lord. *Amen.*

> —*The Student Prayerbook* (Association Press, 1953), p. 19

A PRAYER FOR REPOSE IN GOD

Augustine is a man whose massive intellect has made a tremendous impact on the history of Christendom. Whether we agree with all his doctrinal positions or not, there is no denying his influence. He produced huge volumes which have commanded the attention of scholars for centuries. His *Confessions* is recognized everywhere as one of the classics of devotional and autobiographical literature.

But the thing for which he is best known and will be longest remembered is one sentence found in this prayer: "Thou madest me for Thyself, and my heart is restless until it repose in Thee." This is one of those statements of spiritual genius that are made once in a generation. It lives through the centuries because of its great insight into spiritual truth.

This prayer is significant for another reason; because in the first sentence it summarizes the nature of God and his concern for man. "O Thou Good Omnipotent, Who so carest for everyone of us, as if thou caredst for him alone; and so for all, as if all were but one!" Here is the essence of Christian theology. Here is the basis of the Christian faith: from here one can move on to the better-known statement quoted above.

O Thou Good Omnipotent, Who so carest for everyone of us, as if Thou caredst for him alone; and so for all, as if all were but one! Blessed is the man who loveth Thee, and his friend in Thee, and his enemy for Thee. For he only loses none dear to him, to whom all are dear in Him who cannot be lost. And who is that but our God, the God that made heaven and earth, and filleth them, even by filling them creating them. And Thy law is truth, and truth is Thyself. I behold how some things pass away that others may replace them, but Thou dost never depart, O God, my Father supremely good, Beauty of all things beautiful. To Thee will I intrust whatsoever I have received from Thee, so shall I lose nothing. Thou madest me for Thyself, and my heart is restless until it repose in Thee. *Amen.*

—St. Augustine

A PRAYER FOR DISCIPLINE

St. Ignatius Loyola was a Spanish aristocrat by birth. He spent his boyhood years at the royal court before becoming a soldier, a career he followed until seriously injured in battle. He went through a long and serious emotional struggle. Denied the life of a soldier, disillusioned and unprepared for life at court, he turned to religion as the solution for his personal struggle and his frustrated ambitions. As one historian has said of him, "Unable to live the hard life of a warrior, he would live the even harder life of a saint."

There followed years of struggle with authority, the gaining of an education though much older than most students, the establishment of the Order of the Jesuits with its very strict discipline, and the writing of *Spiritual Exercises*, which is recognized as one of the devotional classics.

Though Ignatius Loyola was a Roman Catholic who lived in the sixteenth century, and though for most Protestants the rigid requirements of the Jesuits seems neither desirable nor necessary, we could all use more discipline in our spiritual lives, and the commitment to service expressed in this prayer still carries a challenge and a goal.

Teach us, good Lord, to serve Thee as Thou deservest; to give and not to count the cost; to fight and not to heed the wounds; to toil and not to seek for rest; to labour and not to ask for any reward, save that of knowing that we do Thy will; through Jesus Christ our Lord. *Amen.*

—St. Ignatius Loyola

A PRAYER FOR PARDON

Dr. Paul Tournier in one of his early books wrote, "There is no worse suffering than a guilty conscience, and certainly none more harmful" (*A Doctor's Casebook in the Light of the Bible*, Harper, 1960, p. 209).

The experience of guilt and the need for forgiveness is common to all men. Every pastor knows this. The psychiatrists know it. The novelists have always known it. Hawthorne showed it in *The Scarlet Letter*, and Shakespeare did in *Macbeth* when he pictured Lady Macbeth walking the floor at night wringing her hands in an act of perpetual futile cleansing.

The Bible is full of prayers for forgiveness. The psalmist said:

Have mercy on me, O God
   according to thy steadfast love;
according to thy abundant mercy
   blot out my transgressions.
Wash me thoroughly from my iniquity,
   and cleanse me from my sin! (Psalm 51:1-2 RSV)

The publican in Jesus' parable of the Pharisee and the publican expressed the feelings of many people when he said, "God, be merciful to me a sinner."

In fact, the Bible says all men should feel this way. "All have sinned, and fall short of the glory of God" (Romans 3:23 RSV). Again, "If we say we have no sin, we deceive ourselves, and the truth is not in us" (1 John 1:8 RSV).

Guilt is a feeling shared by good people as well as bad—by saints as well as sinners. In some cases the saints, because of their great sensitivity, feel more guilt than the sinners.

Because of the pain of which Tournier speaks, men try all sorts of ways to escape the burden of guilt.

Some try to suppress it or, worse, to repress it, to bury it, to deny it exists. Some try to project it onto others. They blame someone else, become overly critical, rationalize their own behavior. Some try to forget it in an endless round of activity, in a mad search for pleasure or in daily good works—or in self-imposed penance. Some just try to endure it, to live with it. None of this works.

Biblically the answer is clear. It is couched in certain ancient, meaningful terms: repentance, confession, restitution, grace, forgiveness, newness of life. That is, one must admit the need, face oneself, and sincerely repent, which literally means "change one's direction." Confession is necessary —confession to God for sure, to others if necessary. Make restitution, correct the wrong you have done; if possible, be willing to forgive others; and finally accept God's grace and be willing to be forgiven.

This can be very complex psychologically and is profoundly theological. As one theologian has said: "The doctrine of forgiveness is the essence of the Christian message. In it, the deepest need of man and the healing grace of God are met."

This prayer, the author of which is unknown, catches up our common need for forgiveness and at the same time the desire to be understanding and compassionate with others.

Forgive me, most gracious Lord and Father, if this day I have done or said anything to increase the pain of the world. Pardon the unkind word, the impatient gesture, the hard and selfish deed, the failure to show sympathy and kindly help where I have had the opportunity but missed it; and enable me so to live that I may daily do something to lessen the tide of human sorrow, and to add to the sum of human happiness; through Him who died for us and rose again, Thy Son, our Saviour, Jesus Christ. *Amen.*

—Author unknown

A PRAYER FOR STRENGTH

Toyohiko Kagawa has been described as the "twentieth-century St. Francis," as "the saint that laughs," as the man in the modern era who has walked most closely in the footsteps of Jesus.

He was born in a nobleman's house, the illegitimate child of one of his father's concubines. His parents died when he was four, and his childhood was lonely and unhappy. Neglected, abused, often humiliated, he seemed to be the victim of circumstances.

Then he was sent to a missionary school to learn English, where he was befriended by a missionary who taught him to read English by reading the Bible.

Here he encountered the stories of Jesus, and his one prayer was "O God, make me like Christ."

Kagawa read widely in the field of social concerns and determined to devote his life to the people of the slums. For this he was disinherited and gave up the fortune that would have been his.

He studied for the ministry while he was living in a six-foot-square shack he had secured in the slums. Here he welcomed all who came. His first applicant had the contagious itch. Kagawa felt it was a test of his commitment.

People left foundlings; others came and beat him up. He contracted tuberculosis, trachoma, and various other ailments, because of the lack of sanitation and the hardships. Because his activities were felt to be subversive, he was imprisoned, an occasion which he used to write a book.

During this period in his life, he wrote some poems published under the title *Songs from the Slums*. One of them is this prayer. The country he alludes to is Japan, but it could be any country.

> Take Thou the burden, Lord;
> I am exhausted with this heavy load.
> My tired hands tremble,
> And I stumble, stumble
>   Along the way.
> Oh, lead with Thine unfailing arm
>   Again today.
>
> Unless Thou lead me, Lord,
> The road I journey on is all too hard.
> Through trust in Thee alone
>   Can I go on.

Yet not for self alone
Thus do I groan;
My people's sorrows are the load I bear.
Lord, hear my prayer—
May Thy strong hand
Strike off all chains
That load my well-loved land.
God, draw her close to Thee!
—Toyohiko Kagawa, *Songs from the Slums* (Abingdon-Cokesbury Press [1935], 1950), p. 89

A PRAYER OF GRATITUDE

Among the most familiar passages read in the Thanksgiving season are the lines from the Hundredth Psalm (v. 4): "Enter into his gates with thanksgiving, and into his courts with praise: be thankful unto him, and bless his name." This praise and thanksgiving was meant to be expressed not just once a year, but all the time.

Not a day should go by but we pause to express our gratitude to God for his goodness. We should remember the common things. We so often forget the beauties of nature, the smile of a child, the handclasp of a friend. We should be grateful for work to do and strength to do it, for the activity of the day and the rest of the night. We should review the great privileges of life, of freedom and beauty and goodness and truth. Above all we should be grateful for God himself, for his goodness, his faithfulness, his forgiveness, and his love.

Over and over the Scriptures urge men to be thankful. In the Old Testament, the psalmist said, "I will give thanks to the Lord with my whole heart" (Psalm 9:1 RSV), and in the New Testament the apostle Paul, though in prison, wrote, "In everything by prayer and supplication with thanksgiving let your requests be made known to God" (Philippians 4:6 RSV).

This prayer of Reinhold Niebuhr is a prayer of gratitude. To it we can add the specific things for which we should be thankful.

We thank Thee, Our Father, for life and love, for the mystery and majesty of existence, for the world of beauty which surrounds us and for the miracle of our conscious life by which we behold the wonders of the universe.

We thank Thee for the glimpses of nobility in human life which redeem it from sordidness and reassure us that thy image is in the heart of man. We are grateful for the ties which bind us to our fellow-men; for our common toil in industry and marts of trade; for our joint inheritance as citizens of this nation; for traditions and customs hallowed by age through which our passions are ordered and channelled; for the love of beauty and truth and goodness by which we transcend the chasms of race and nation; for the faith of our fathers by which we claim kinship with the past and gain strength for the present; for the love of dear ones in our homes and for the enlarging responsibilities and sobering duties of our family life; for the serenity of old people who redeem us of fretfulness and for the faith and courage of youth through which we are saved from sloth.

We are not worthy of the rich inheritances of our common life. We confess that we have profaned the temple of this life by our selfishness and heedlessness. We have sought to gain advantage of our brothers who are bound together with us by many different ties. Have mercy upon us that we may express our gratitude for thy many mercies by contrition for our sins and that we may prove our repentance by lives dedicated more fully to thee and to the common good, through Jesus Christ our Lord. *Amen.*

—Reinhold Niebuhr, quoted in
Prayers for Services, pp. 80-81

FROM
THE BOOK OF COMMON PRAYER

Some prayers by the very nature of their expression speak to all men and all generations. This is true of this prayer from *The Book of Common Prayer* which is found in most collections of prayers. It is ascribed to Bishop Leofric, who lived in the eleventh century, and it has been a source of inspiration to thousands of people. One would do well to memorize it and repeat it over and over and over again.

One could use it as a basis of meditation, repeating a phrase and then meditating on its deep meaning until it becomes a part of oneself. One could read it, pausing at each punctuation mark and meditating on the previous phrase before going on. It was written for public worship, with a congregation, but if one changes the pronouns from "our" and "we" to "my" and "I" it becomes a very deep personal prayer.

Almighty God, unto whom all hearts are open, all desires known, and from whom no secrets are hid; Cleanse the thoughts of our hearts by inspiration of Thy Holy Spirit, that we may perfectly love Thee, and worthily magnify Thy Holy Name; through Christ our Lord. *Amen.*
—Bishop Leofric (1050) from
The Book of Common Prayer

A PRAYER FOR COURAGE

Martin Luther faced public ridicule, vocational failure, opposition, physical danger, excommunication. Yet in the presence of all this he said, "It is neither safe nor right to go against one's conscience. Here I stand, I can do no other, so help me God."

Such courage comes only through faith. Once when he was on trial for his very life, when all he had hoped and stood for seemed to be crashing around his head, a man taunted him with the question "When all men forsake you, where will you find refuge?" Luther is reported to have answered quickly, "Under heaven."

Prayer, sometimes mistakenly considered the refuge of the weak, is actually the ultimate resource of the strong. Men like Martin Luther, David Livingstone, Adoniram Judson, and Wilfred Grenfell were men of courage. They were also men of prayer.

It was at a time of great personal danger, when the opposition was the bitterest, when the feudal lords of Germany opposed him and the Church with all its influence was arrayed against him, that Luther prayed this prayer:

O Thou, my God! Do Thou, my God, stand by me, against all the world's wisdom and reason. Oh, do it! Thou must do it! Yea, Thou alone must do it! Not mine, but Thine, is the cause. For my own self, I have nothing to do with these great and earthly lords. I would prefer to have peaceful days, and to be out of this turmoil. But Thine, O Lord, is this cause; it is righteous and eternal. Stand by me, Thou true Eternal God! In no man do I trust. All that is of the flesh and savours of the flesh is here of no account. God, O God! dost Thou not hear me, O my God? Art Thou dead? No. Thou canst not die; Thou art only hiding Thyself. Hast Thou chosen me for this work? I ask Thee how I may be sure of this, if it be Thy will; for I would never have thought, in all my life, of undertaking aught against such great lords. Stand by me, O God, in the Name of Thy dear Son, Jesus Christ, who shall be my Defence and Shelter, yea, my Mighty Fortress, through the might and strength of Thy Holy Spirit. God help me. *Amen.*

—Martin Luther

FROM DOUBT TO FAITH

Horace Bushnell was a man of great faith. Through his books and sermons, he has helped many others find faith. His sermon "Every Man's Life a Plan of God" was described by one authority in homiletics as one of the three greatest sermons ever preached in America.

When he was invited to preach in the chapel at Yale, he chose as his subject "The Dissolving of Doubts." It was received with great appreciation because students then as now were struggling with doubt.

There is a story behind that sermon. When he was a tutor in the law school at Yale, years before, a revival of religious interest spread across the campus. All the students seemed to be caught up in it, except Bushnell's. Bushnell himself went through a period, as he later said, when he experienced "agonies of mental darkness concerning God."

He didn't know what he believed, but he felt a moral responsibility to his students. Although he had many questions and much uncertainty, he determined to begin with what he knew and move from there.

In spite of his doubts, he knew that

> love was better than hate,
> honesty was better than dishonesty,
> purity was better than impurity,
> loyalty was better than treachery.

He would hold to those things of which he was sure, live by what he knew and at the same time carry on an earnest quest for more understanding. He was expressing the same emotions and the same desire as the man who said to Jesus, "I believe; help my unbelief!" (Mark 9:24 RSV).

Out of the struggle, after much time and effort, he attained the faith that led him from law to the ministry, from doubt to faith, from skepticism to trust. Faith is often spoken of as a necessity for prayer. It is also true that prayer is necessary for faith.

In the midst of Bushnell's intellectual quest was a sense of commitment when he prayed this prayer:

O God, I believe there is an eternal difference between right and wrong, and I hereby give myself up to do the right and refrain from the wrong. I believe that Thou dost exist, and if Thou canst hear my prayer and will reveal Thyself to me, I pledge myself to do Thy will, and I make that pledge fully, freely and forever. *Amen.*

—Horace Bushnell

A PRAYER OF INTERCESSION

If our prayer life is to be complete, it must include not only prayers for ourselves, but prayers for others. When Jean Frédéric Oberlin was having such a successful ministry in the Vosges Mountains in France, he used to spend an hour a day on his knees, praying for his people, one by one, by name. His people knew it and passed his house in silence during this hour. It is no wonder he had such a fine ministry.

Jesus prayed for his friends; he prayed for his disciples; he even prayed for his enemies; he prayed for the whole world.

We should include the whole world in our prayers. This prayer of Reinhold Niebuhr's can guide and stimulate us to offer our own prayer for "all sorts and conditions of men":

O God, who hast made us a royal priesthood that we might offer unto thee prayer and intercession for all sorts and conditions of men, hear us as we pray;

For all who toil in the burden and the heat of the day that they may enjoy the rewards of their industry, that they may not be defrauded of their due and that we may never cease to be mindful of our debt to them, remembering with gratitude the multitude of services which must be performed to make our life tolerable;

For those who have authority and power over their fellowmen, that they may not use it for selfish advantage but be guided to do justice and to love mercy;

For those who have been worsted in the battles of life, whether by the inhumanity of their fellows, their own limitations or the fickleness of fortune, that they may contend against injustice without bitterness, overcome their own weaknesses with diligence and learn how to accept what cannot be altered, with patience;

For the rulers of nations that they may act wisely and without pride, and seek to promote peace among the peoples and establish justice in our common life;

For the teachers and ministers of the word, for artists and interpreters of our spiritual life that they may rightly divide the word of truth and not be tempted by pride or greed or any ignoble passion to corrupt the truth to which they are committed;

For prophets and seers and saints who awaken us from our sloth that they may continue to hold their torches high in a world darkened by prejudice and sin and never be disobedient to the heavenly vision;

O God, who hast bound us together in this bundle of

life, give us the grace to understand how our lives depend upon the courage, the industry, the honesty and the integrity of our fellowmen, that we may be mindful of their needs, grateful for their faithfulness and faithful in our responsibilities to them, through Jesus Christ our Lord. Amen.

> —Reinhold Niebuhr, quoted in *Prayers for Services*, pp. 144-45

A PHILOSOPHY OF LIFE

Sometimes a whole philosophy of life can be expressed in a few words or phrases. W. E. Orchard has put into the four sentences of this prayer sufficient wisdom to guide and direct a life in the way of truth and love and faith. One could well read it, and re-read it, meditate upon it—and then pray it until it becomes one's own.

It is a request for a love of truth, for responsibility in fulfilling one's duty, and for penitence that one may have strength, light, wisdom, cleansing, and fellowship with God.

O God, in whom we live and move and have our being, enable us to feel the strength that surrounds us, to follow the light that indwells us, and to avail ourselves of the wisdom Thou givest liberally to all who ask of Thee.

Give to us so great a love of truth that we may pass beyond all doubt and error, until our minds are stayed on Thee, and our thoughts are kept in perfect peace.

Give us wisdom to follow the promptings of duty in our daily lives, that we may grow conscious of Thy presence who workest hitherto, and callest us to be fellow-workers now with Thee.

Grant unto us the grace of penitence that we may not grow insensible to our need of forgiveness, from one another, and from Thee; but seek cleansing in communion, fellowship in the light, and rest upon Thy heart. *Amen.*

—W. E. Orchard, *The Temple* (Dutton, 1918), p. 60

A PRAYER FOR QUIETNESS
AND TRUST

Some of the world's greatest expressions of prayer are found in the hymnbook. All too often we don't think of them as prayers when we sing them in congregational worship (in fact, congregational singing is sometimes done routinely without much thought or identification with the words at all), but that is what they were intended to be. Indeed, many of the great hymns were first of all written as prayers and were only later set to music.

No hymn or prayer better expresses man's needs than does John Greenleaf Whittier's "Dear Lord and Father of Mankind."

Whittier was a Quaker. Perhaps only a Quaker could have written the words

> Drop thy still dews of quietness,
> Till all our strivings cease.

Is anything more relevant to man and his needs today?

> Take from our souls the strain and stress,
> And let our ordered lives confess
> The beauty of thy peace."

This Quaker emphasis on the value of silence is something we all need. In the midst of the stress and turmoil of the present-day world we need the serenity and calm that comes only in the silence, when we can hear "the still, small voice."

One should point out, however, that this is not the counsel of one who would escape the world and its responsibilities and retreat into silence. Whittier's was no isolated or protected life. He was active in the antislavery movement and demonstrated great courage as he challenged the evils of his day. He knew that if he was to carry on such activities he also needed solitude to gain some inner peace.

He also expressed the need for simple trust in Christ and his Spirit. The verse

> In simple trust like theirs who heard
> Beside the Syrian sea,
> The gracious calling of the Lord
> Let us, like them, without a word
> Rise up and follow thee.

anticipates the words with which Albert Schweitzer concluded his *Quest of the Historical Jesus:* "He comes to us as one unknown without a name, as of old, by the lakeside, He comes to those who knew Him not. He speaks to us the same word, 'Follow thou me!' and sets us to the tasks which He has to fulfill for our time. He commands. And to those who obey Him, whether they be wise or simple, He will reveal Himself in the toils, the conflicts, the sufferings which they shall pass through in His fellowship, and as an ineffable mystery, they shall learn in their own experience who He is."

Whether one sings Whittier's words in corporate worship, or meditates on their meaning by oneself, one should see them as a prayer.

> Dear Lord and Father of mankind,
> Forgive our foolish ways;
> Reclothe us in our rightful mind,
> In purer lives thy service find,
> In deeper reverence, praise.
>
> In simple trust like theirs who heard,
> Beside the Syrian sea,
> The gracious calling of the Lord,
> Let us, like them, without a word
> Rise up and follow thee.
>
> O sabbath rest by Galilee!
> O calm of hills above,
> Where Jesus knelt to share with thee
> The silence of eternity,
> Interpreted by love!
>
> Drop thy still dews of quietness,
> Till all our strivings cease;

Take from our souls the strain and stress,
And let our ordered lives confess
The beauty of thy peace.

Breathe through the heats of our desire
Thy coolness and thy balm;
Let sense be dumb, let flesh retire:
Speak through the earthquake, wind, and fire,
O still, small voice of calm.

—John Greenleaf Whittier

A PRAYER FOR HUMILITY

Humility is often mistakenly seen as weakness. In the Bible it is a sign of strength. Charles Kingsley in the prayer below saw it as a source of power.

Pride was recognized as one of the seven deadly sins in the Middle Ages, and not without reason. In the Old Testament we read:

> Pride goes before destruction,
> and a haughty spirit before a fall.
> (Proverbs 16:18 RSV)

On more than one occasion Jesus said that everyone who exalts himself will be humbled, but he who humbles himself will be exalted (Matthew 18:4, 23:12; Luke 14:11, 18:14).

In the parable of the Pharisee and the publican he

pictured two men in marked contrast. The Pharisee was a good man in many respects, certainly a religious man, but one whose pride caused him to parade his virtue and whose self-righteousness caused him to look down on other men. The publican, by contrast, a sinner by his own admission, was commended for his honesty, sincerity, and humility.

Perhaps true humility can only be attained through prayer, like that of the publican, "God, be merciful to me a sinner" (Luke 18:13 RSV), or the prayer which follows, which has as the center of its request a desire for the old-time virtues of gentleness, simplicity, and humility.

Take from us, O Lord, all pride and vanity, all boasting and forwardness, and give us the true courage that shows itself by gentleness, the true wisdom that shows itself by simplicity, and the true power that shows itself by humility; through Jesus Christ our Lord. *Amen.*

—Charles Kingsley

O LOVE THAT WILT NOT LET ME GO

George Matheson was one of Scotland's greatest preachers. Though he made some significant contributions to the world's devotional literature, he is probably best known for his hymn "O Love That Wilt Not Let Me Go."

He became totally blind while still a student at the University of Glasgow, but in spite of this handicap he finished his degree, and went on to preach, with great success, first at Innellan and then at St. Bernard's Parish Church in Edinburgh. He attracted large crowds because of the power of his preaching, for which both the text and the sermon had to be memorized beforehand. Some who heard him, testify also to the moving influence of his prayers.

PRAYER-BASED GROWTH GROUPS

The prayer that follows picks up some of the themes found in his famous hymn. He himself said that this hymn, which was written some twenty years after his blindness, came out of a period of great personal struggle. It came to him all at once, as a unit, and was autobiographical in nature. He did "trace the rainbow through the rain." This prayer too is autobiographical. It contains a confident expression which opens doors of understanding into the deep devotional nature of Matheson's own life.

O Thou divine Spirit that, in all events of life, art knocking at the door of my heart, help me to respond to Thee. I would not be driven blindly as the stars over their courses. I would not be made to work out Thy will unwillingly, to fulfill Thy law unintelligently, to obey Thy mandates unsympathetically. I would take the events of my life as good and perfect gifts from Thee; I would receive even the sorrows of life as disguised gifts from Thee. I would have my heart open at all times to receive—at morning, noon, and night; in spring, and summer, and winter. Whether Thou comest to me in sunshine or in rain, I would take Thee into my heart joyfully. Thou art Thyself more than the sunshine, Thou art Thyself compensation for the rain; it is Thee and not Thy gifts I crave; knock, and I shall open unto Thee. *Amen.*

—George Matheson

THE TESTIMONY OF
THE CENTURIES

Emerson said of Jesus, "He took His stride from the centuries rather than from the hours." Centuries before the time of Christ the psalmist in a period of great personal discouragement said, "Our fathers trusted in thee and thou didst deliver them" (Psalm 22:4). As he reflected back over the generations and recalled how his fathers had trusted and gained strength, so he knew the God of his fathers was his God as well.

The author of the Epistle to the Hebrews in a time of persecution, after defining faith as "the assurance of things hoped for, the conviction of things not seen," said "by it the men of old received divine approval" (11:1-2 RSV). Then he went on to list the heroes of the faith and to describe the courage of their acts. They too took their stride from the centuries rather than from the hours.

To do this takes an act of faith. It is expressed in the oft-quoted lines

> Truth forever on the scaffold,
>   Wrong forever on the throne—
> Yet that scaffold sways the future,
>   and, behind the dim unknown,
> Standeth God within the shadow,
>   keeping watch above his own.

It is this faith in the God of the past, who is also the God of the future, that is expressed in this prayer. Since he is a God of the past and also of the future he is a source of strength and courage for the present.

O God, who art, and wast, and art to come, before whose face the generations rise and pass away; age after age the living seek Thee, and find that of Thy faithfulness there is no end. Our fathers in their pilgrimage walked by Thy guidance, and rested on Thy compassion; still to their children be Thou the cloud by day, the fire by night. In our manifold temptations, Thou alone knowest and art ever nigh: in sorrow, Thy pity revives the fainting soul; in our prosperity and ease, it is Thy Spirit only that can wean us from our pride and keep us low. O Thou sole Source of peace and righteousness! take now the veil from every heart; and join us in one communion with Thy prophets and saints who have trusted in Thee, and were not ashamed. Not of our worthiness, but of Thy tender mercy, hear our prayer. *Amen*.

—James Martineau

A MORNING PRAYER

Most authorities on prayer and the devotional life agree that the first thing in the morning is one of the best times to pray. It sets the tone for the whole day.

Apparently Jesus began his days in this manner. "And in the morning, a great while before day, he rose and went out to a lonely place, and there he prayed" (Mark 1:35 RSV).

William Barclay is a great biblical scholar. He is Professor of Divinity and Biblical Criticism at Glasgow University and has written many authoritative books on the Bible. He has also prepared several books of prayers including one called *A Guide to Daily Prayer*. This little book includes a series of prayers for both morning and evening. This one,

PRAYER-BASED GROWTH GROUPS

which is the first one in the book, expresses thoughts which would apply to most people:

> Help me, O God, to meet in the right way and in the right spirit everything which comes to me to-day.
> Help me to approach my work cheerfully, and my tasks diligently.
> Help me to meet people courteously, and, if need be, to suffer fools gladly.
> Help me to meet disappointments, frustrations, hindrances, opposition, calmly and without irritation.
> Help me to meet delays with patience, and unreasonable demands with self-control.
> Help me to accept praise modestly, and criticism without losing my temper.
> Keep me serene all through to-day.
> All this I ask for Jesus' sake. *Amen.*
> —William Barclay, *A Guide to Daily Prayer*, p. 20

AN EVENING INVOCATION

"And after he had dismissed the crowds, he went up on the mountain by himself to pray. When evening came, he was there alone" (Matthew 14:23-24 RSV)—such was the manner in which Jesus closed the day. What took place in these moments of solitude we do not know, but they were spent in prayer. Here was a source of his serenity and strength.

After the day's work and activity is done, we too need to pray. We need to be conscious of the nearness of God. Here is a prayer that will guide us as we offer our own prayer of confidence and trust:

Lord of the evening hour, who hast often met with us at the close of day, be our refuge now from the noise of the world and the care of our own spirits. Grant us thy peace. Let not the darkness of our ignorance and folly, of our sorrow and sin hide thee from us. Draw near to us that we may be near to thee. Speak to each of us the word that we need, and let thy word abide in us till it has wrought in us thy holy will. Quicken and refresh our hearts, renew and increase our strength so that we may grow into the likeness of thy faithful children and by our worship at this time be enabled better to serve thee in our daily life in the spirit of Jesus Christ our Lord. *Amen.*

—John Hunter

A PASTORAL PRAYER

Harry Emerson Fosdick, who is most well known as a preacher, was persuaded late in his ministry to publish some of his pastoral prayers. In the introduction he defined his own philosophy of prayer in these words: "In non-liturgical churches, the minister does not kneel in the chancel, facing the altar, as though addressing himself to the Most High. He stands in the pulpit, facing the congregation. That obvious fact defines his function in public prayer. He is trying so to phrase the soul's adoration, thanksgiving, penitence, petitions, and intercessions, that the people may be caught up into his prayer, and may themselves pray with him.

"This requires two things. Preparation, spiritual

awareness and a deep sensitivity to human need on the part of the pastor. It demands receptivity and a prayerful spirit on the part of the parishioners. When these two are combined, then results can take place."

For the pastor, this is "a sacred, soul-searching task. It calls for deep and sympathetic insight into human need, for sensitive awareness of both individual and social problems, and for faith in God's grace and mercy; and it demands dedicated and careful preparation as much as does the preaching of a sermon" (*A Book of Public Prayers*, pp. 7-8).

George Buttrick said, "If the minister had to choose between prayer and sermon, he might better forget the sermon" (*Prayer*, p. 269). (Fortunately, he doesn't have to make that choice.)

Here is an example of a pastoral prayer that demonstrates these qualities—deep spiritual awareness and deep personal concerns:

Eternal Spirit, who carest for each of us as if thou hadst none else to care for, and yet carest for all even as thou carest for each, we turn our hearts to thee. All our thoughts touch but the outskirts of thy ways; our imaginations are but partial pictures of thy truth; our words concerning thee are short plummets dropped into a deep sea. Yet into thy sanctuary we come with grateful and expectant hearts, because while we, by searching, cannot find thee out, thou, by thy searching, canst find us.

Spirit of the living God, discover us today. Come through the tangled pathways, grown with weed and thicket, that have kept thee from us. We cannot reach to thee; reach thou to us, that some soul, who came here barren of thy grace, may go out, singing, O God, thou art my God!

Discover us in conscience. Let some moral imperative be laid upon our souls today. Save us from our evasions and deceits, and the soft complacency with which we excuse ourselves, and let some ennobling word of justice and beauty come to us today. Be stern with us, O living God, and chasten us by strong guidance in righteousness.

Discover us through the experience of forgiveness. Thou seest how many sins here have never been made right—barbed words spoken that hurt another, never atoned for, and still unforgiven; wrongs done against thy laws and man's good, and no pardon sought, no restitution made. Grant us the salvation of thy forgiveness, and the pardon of those whom we have wronged. May some fellowship gone awry be put straight today; may some broken relationships be restored to integrity; may some storm-tossed souls find thy peace.

Come to us in the spirit of dedication. Never great until we confront something loftier than our own lives, never happy while we are self-centered, we seek our salvation in thee. Bring thou within our ken some purpose worth living for; remind us of some whom we can help, some cause that we can serve. May we forget ourselves into character and usefulness, because thou hast sought us out.

Come to us in the experience of inner power. We ask not for easy lives, but for adequacy. We ask not to be freed from storms, but to have houses built on rock that will not fall. We pray not for a smooth sea, but for a stout ship, a good compass, and a strong heart to sail. O God, discover us with the resources of thy power, that we may be strong within.

We pray for our unhappy world in all its wretchedness and violence. See how our sins have wrecked the peace of mankind, divided us into warring nations and hostile races, and made so unequal man's comfort and estate that the world is rent by envy and ill will. Come thou to thy wayward humanity, all of us thy children, one family with one Father, trying ruinously to be something that we are not, enemies when we should be brothers. Bring the Spirit of the Christ into our hearts, we humbly beseech thee.

On all soldiers of the common good let thy blessing rest. From housewives in the kitchen to presidents and kings in their high stations, we pray for all, in ordinary or extraordinary places, who serve their fellows. Upon physicians and nurses, lawyers and teachers, business-men and statesmen, upon all who work for the poor and bear on their hearts vicariously the burdens of unhappy folk forgotten by the world, we ask thy blessing. Upon all those who work for the purification of our politics, the bringing in of world peace, and the spread of the Gospel of the Son of Man we pray.

Help us all so inwardly to conduct our own lives that whether we live in prosperity or misfortune we, too, may be among the honorable company of thy true servants who lift the world and do not lean upon it, and who leave it a better place in which thou mayest rear thy human family.

We ask it in the Spirit of Christ. *Amen*.

—Harry Emerson Fosdick,
A Book of Public Prayers
(Harper, 1959, pp. 12-13)

III
APPENDIXES

The material in the appendixes is supplementary material that can be used in connection with the growth group idea, and bibliographies that provide further reading on the two ideas that are united here—prayer and group procedures.

RELAXATION TRAINING

There is a proverb which says, "You will break the bow if you keep it always stretched." Though the words are from ancient times, the application is needed now. Many people are stretched to the breaking point.

Jesus, at a very busy time in his ministry, said to his disciples, "Come ye yourselves apart . . . and rest awhile" (Mark 6:31). Not many sermons are preached on that text, but the suggestion Jesus made to his followers is needed advice for many people today.

God gave us the power to work and to strive. He also gave us the power to rest and relax. Our culture has placed all its emphasis on the first. Cultivating the power of the latter may help us work more effectively.

Relaxation is a skill which must be learned. We have learned how to be tense. We need to learn how to relax. The two are contradictory to each other: you can't be tense and relaxed at the same time.

Tension is a habit. It has been learned by thousands of repetitions over and over and over again. One meets and solves a difficult situation with tension, then another and another until the automatic response is one of tension. This becomes chronic, resulting in fatigue, nervousness, and continued tension.

Many people try to go "apart and rest," but find they can't rest. The tension is too much of a habitual response. The habit of tension must be unlearned; to correct a habit, develop a better one. Much study and research has been done in this problem. Relaxation can be learned. Tension can be reduced.

Dr. Edmund Jacobson of the University of Chicago has made a lifelong study of the phenomenon of relaxation. His book *You Must Relax* (McGraw-Hill, 1957) cites many instances of physical ills that were corrected when his patients learned to relax. Joseph Wolpe, the psychotherapist, teaches all his patients to relax. They come to him because of tension. He trains them to relax in the same situations that caused the tension.

Relaxation relieves tension; it reduces anxiety; it restores energy; it increases strength; it improves efficiency; it makes possible greater effort.

A famous athlete being interviewed during a World Series was asked what was the secret of playing well under great pressure. He replied, "The ability to relax." What is true of athletics is true in almost every other area.

To propose relaxation is not to advocate diminishing of effort. Relaxation is to help a person increase his efforts and be more effective. One needs alternative periods of activity—at times intense activity—with periods of rest and relaxation. After all, according to the book of Genesis, even God rested one day out of seven.

Those who have made a study of relaxation point out certain things:

—For some people, the solution is easy. They are not particularly tense. The simple admonition to "rest awhile" may be all they need.

—For others it is more difficult. Tension is their natural response. Relaxation must be learned and developed. For such persons definite, regular procedures may be necessary.

—The reading of Jacobson's book may help these people understand the principles and nature of relaxation. Jacobson says it quite simply: Relaxation is the opposite of effort.

—All authorities agree that learning to relax may take several weeks, even months. Jacobson suggests weeks of training. Others feel less time is necessary. Since habits of long standing are being unlearned, it will take time to develop new ones.

—This makes it obvious that relaxation involves the scheduling of time and discipline. Time must be found to relax the tension. It must be done regularly and with perseverance. Some advocate fifteen minutes a day (or better, twice a day) for nothing but relaxation.

—Try this exercise as an experiment for a month. Set aside a fifteen-minute period twice a day to train yourself to relax. Select a place that is quiet, free from distractions or probable interruptions. Place yourself in a comfortable position. Lying down is best, although it can be done in a comfortable chair. Tighten the muscles of the jaw by bringing the teeth together. This is tension. Let the jaw drop limp. This is relaxation. Get the "feeling" of relaxation. These preliminary exercises can be dropped after the first few days. With the body in a comfortable position, breathe in deeply, hold for four counts, exhale and hold for four counts, do nothing for four counts. Repeat five times. Then begin your exercise in progressive relaxation by concentrating on each part of the body until it is completely relaxed. Starting with the scalp and forehead let them go until they are smooth and relaxed. Move slowly to the eyes and facial muscles. Let them go completely relaxed. Think of the tongue and cheeks until they are relaxed. Now the neck and throat; let them go completely relaxed. Across the shoulders and down the spine, let them go until they are relaxed. You should be breathing deeply and easily now. Next go down the arms, first the upper arm, the elbows, then slowly move to the forearm, the wrists, the hands, the fingers. Now the abdominal region, the whole intestinal tract, let it all go, deep inside. Next the legs. First the thighs, down to the knees, the calves, the ankles, the feet and toes. Now, go over the entire body, let it all go, completely relaxed. If any tension continues, focus on that part until it is relaxed. Gradually this will become easier and you will become more relaxed at other times as well as when you are doing the exercises.

In a sense, rest and relaxation are religious experiences. Some persons use modifications of the above exercises prior to meditation and prayer. To rest and relax is an act of faith.

In returning and rest you shall be saved;
in quietness and in trust shall be your strength.
(Isaiah 30:15 RSV)

FREE WRITING

John Woolman, John Wesley, and John R. Mott were men of great spiritual depth and power who had one thing in common: they kept a journal, a diary, or a notebook wherein they recorded their deepest thoughts and concerns. How much this practice contributed to their insight, to their self-understanding, to the attainment of their goals, we do not know; but it seems that it had great practical value. Undoubtedly Augustine received significant personal help from writing his *Confessions*, as Pascal did in recording his *Thoughts*.

Some people who are not so famous have found that writing helps. In *On Listening to Another* (Harper, 1955, p. 55), Douglas V. Steere tells of an early Quaker saint, Henry Hodgkins, who took the first hour of each morning for a period of prayer followed by biblical or devotional reading and then a spell of "writing his heart out." No one saw that writing, but it enabled Hodgkins to clarify some of the insights that came to him from his reading and meditation.

Many people, when confronted with a decision, have found that listing the pros and cons on a piece of paper helps them weigh the alternatives. Some have found that it is an aid in their devotional lives if they write out their prayers.

Counselors have found that it is a good supplement to counseling sessions to have a counselee write out his feelings.

Fred McKinney, in his book *Counseling for Personal Adjustment in Schools and Colleges* advises that persons who are troubled with a problem, or who are seeking growth in character and personality, should practice what he calls "free writing." This consists simply in expressing on paper whatever one's thoughts or feelings are. He says it is quite effective in time of tension. McKinney advises persons to write in any way they wish, as rapidly as they can, until the tension is reduced and some understanding is secured. He writes:

The important aspect of this project is that it is completely free. Allow every idea and feeling that comes to you to arise, and write at least some of it down. No one has to read it, not even you. You don't have to put into action what you write down. In fact, often after you express a feeling it is no longer strong. You may feel different after strongly expressing an attitude. You may, and probably should, tear up or burn what you write after writing it. If the end result of this free expression is relaxation and a few clear ideas about yourself and your plans, then it has been effective. (*Counseling for Personal Adjustment in Schools and Colleges,* Houghton Mifflin, 1958, p. 45)

Phillips and Wiener in their book *Short-Term Psychotherapy and Structured Behavior Change* (McGraw-Hill, 1966) include a discussion of what they call "writing therapy." They describe how it has been used in a college counseling clinic to meet the pressures of a waiting list. When a counselor does not have time to see all the clients seeking help, he has some write out their problems. The counselor then evaluates and comments on the written-out problems. While no adequate research exists as yet, there have been very favorable results.

There seems to be little question that for those so motivated, personal growth, new insights, and deeper understanding can come as a result of such processes.

The following guidelines are suggested:

1. Set a time and place to do the writing, and keep it faithfully like any other appointment.

2. Continue over a fairly extended period of time. Results can come quickly, but they are more likely to come after some time.

3. Do not worry about penmanship, grammar, or punctuation. This is an experiment in free expression, not authorship.

4. Be frank, honest, and specific. It does no good to evade issues.

5. Include your concerns and problems, but also your goals and aspirations.

6. If you are seeing a counselor, share what you have written with him. If not, destroy it when you have completed it; or keep it to study, but where it will not be found by others.

7. Be positive. Never complete a statement without listing some of your strengths.

8. When you have completed a statement, lay it aside; return to your tasks or pleasures with new freedom.

Bibliography

BOOKS ON GROUP WORK

The following list is a bibliography of some of the basic books on the group process, group counseling, and group guidance. Anyone wishing to be an effective group leader would want to be familiar with the principles and procedures they describe.

This list was compiled with the assistance of Dr. Marcus Bryant of the Department of Pastoral Care, Brite Divinity School, Texas Christian University, who is a specialist in the group process.

Bales, Robert F. *et al. Small Groups: Studies in Social Interaction.* Rev. ed. New York: Knopf, 1965.

Berne, Eric. *The Structure and Dynamics of Organizations and Groups. 1963; New York: Ballantine Books, 1973.*

Casteel, John L. *The Creative Role of Interpersonal Groups in the Church Today. New York: Association Press, 1968.*

————*Spiritual Renewal Through Personal Groups.* New York: Association Press, 1957.

Clinebell, Howard. *The People Dynamic.* New York: Harper & Row, 1972.

Driver, Helen I., and contributors. *Counseling and Learning Through Small-Group Discussion.* Madison, Wis.: Monona-Driver Book Co., 1958.

Durkin, Helen E. *The Group in Depth.* New York: International Universities Press, 1966.

Goldberg, Carl. *Encounter: Group Sensitivity Training Experience.* New York: Science House, 1971.

Howe, Reuel L. *The Miracle of Dialogue.* New York: The Seabury Press, 1963.

Knowles, Joseph W. *Group Counseling.* Philadelphia: Fortress Press (1964), 1967.

Leslie, Robert C. *Sharing Groups in the Church.* Nashville: Abingdon Pres, 1970.

Luft, Joseph, *Group Processes: An Introduction to Group Dynamics.* Palo Alto, Calif.: National Press Books, 1970.

Maclennan, Beryce W., and Naomi Felsenfeld. *Group*

Counseling and Psychotherapy with Adolescents. New York: Columbia University Press, 1968.

Malamud, Daniel I., and Solomon Machover. *Toward Self-Understanding: Group Techniques in Self-Confrontation.* Springfield, Ill.: Charles C. Thomas (1965), 1970.

Miles, Matthew. *Learning to Work in Groups.* New York: Teachers College, Columbia University, 1959.

Mowrer, O. H. *The New Group Therapy.* New York: Van Nostrand Reinhold Co., 1964.

Oden, Thomas C. *The Intensive Group Experience: The New Pietism.* Philadelphia: The Westminster Press, 1972.

Ohlsen, Merle M. *Group Counseling.* New York: Holt, Rinehart and Winston, 1970.

Olmsted, Michael S. *The Small Group.* New York: Random House, 1959.

Pastoral Psychology. Special issues on small groups, April, 1955; June, 1964.

Raines, Robert A. *New Life in the Church.* New York: Harper & Brothers, 1961.

Reid, Clyde. *Groups Alive–Church Alive.* New York: Harper & Row, 1969.

Rogers, Carl. *Carl Rogers on Encounter Groups.* New York: Harper & Row, 1970.

BOOKS FOR UNDERSTANDING TRANSACTIONAL ANALYSIS

Berne, Eric. *Games People Play.* New York: Grove Press, 1964.

————. *What Do You Say After You Say Hello?* New York: Grove Press, 1972.

Harris, Thomas A. *I'm OK—You're OK.* New York: Harper & Row, 1969.

James, Muriel, and Dorothy Jongeward. *Born to Win.* Reading, Mass.: Addison-Wesley Press, 1971.

BOOKS ON PRAYER

The program described in this volume is a discussion of prayers, not a discussion of prayer. However, since it is based on prayers it is quite natural that a discussion of the theories and methods of prayer itself would result. The following books tell how men and women have thought about prayer. The leader of a growth group might wish to familiarize himself with some of them.

Bowden, Guy. *The Dazzling Darkness.* 1950; London: Seraph Books, 1963.

Buttrick, George. *Prayer.* Nashville: Abingdon-Cokesbury Press, 1942.

————. *The Power of Prayer Today.* Waco, Tex.: Word Books, 1973.

Cant, Reginald. *Heart in Pilgrimage.* New York: Harper & Brothers, 1961.

Coburn, John. *Prayer and Personal Religion.* Philadelphia: The Westminster Press, 1957.

Eaton, Kenneth O. *Men Who Talked with God.* Nashville: Abingdon Press, 1964.

Fosdick, Harry Emerson. *The Meaning of Prayer.* New York: Association Press (1915), 1962.

Garrett, Constance. *Growth in Prayer.* New York: The Macmillan Co., 1950.

Harkness, Georgia. *Prayer and the Common Life.* Nashville: Abingdon-Cokesbury Press, 1948.

Heard, Gerald. *Ten Questions in Prayer.* Wallingford, Pa.: Pendle Hill, 1951.

Herman, E. *Creative Prayer.* 1925; Greenwood, S.C.: Attic Press, 1953.

Jackson, Edgar. *Understanding Prayer.* New York: World Publishing Co. 1968.

Kimmel, Jo. *Steps to Prayer Power.* Nashville: Abingdon Press, 1972.

Laubach, Frank. *Prayer, the Mightiest Force in the World.* Old Tappan, N.J.: Fleming H. Revell, n.d.

Lester, Muriel. *Ways of Praying.* 1932; Nashville: Abingdon Press, 1962.

Lewis, C. S. *Letters to Malcolm: Chiefly on Prayer.* New York: Harcourt Brace Jovanovich, 1964.

Magee, John. *Reality and Prayer.* Nashville: Abingdon Press, 1969.

Parker, William R., and E. St. Johns. *Prayer Can Change Your Life.* New York: Prentice-Hall, 1957.

Pittenger, W. Norman. *God's Way with Men.* Valley Forge, Pa.: Judson Press, 1970.

Radcliffe, Lynn. *Making Prayer Real.* Nashville:

BIBLIOGRAPHY

Abingdon-Cokesbury Press, 1952.

Whiston, Charles. *Teach Us to Pray.* Boston: Pilgrim Press, 1949.

Yungblut, John R. *Rediscovering Prayer.* New York: The Seabury Press, 1972.

BOOKS OF PRAYERS

Baillie, John. *A Diary of Private Prayer.* New York: Charles Scribner's Sons, 1949.

Barclay, William. *Book of Everyday Prayers.* New York: Harper & Brothers, 1960.

―――. *A Guide to Daily Prayer.* New York: Harper & Row, 1962.

Beecher, Henry Ward. *Prayers from Plymouth Pulpit.* London: Hodder & Stoughton, 1967.

Blackwood, Andrew et al. *Prayers for All Occasions.* Grand Rapids, Mich.: Baker Book House, n.d.

Bowie, Walter R. *Lift Up Your Hearts.* Nashville: Abingdon Press, 1956.

Boyd, Malcolm. *Are You Running With Me, Jesus?* 1965; New York: Avon Books, 1972.

Carr, Jo, and Imogene Sorley. *Bless This Mess and Other Prayers.* Nashville: Abingdon Press, 1969.

Donne, John. *Prayers.* Edited by Herbert H. Umbach. New Haven: College and University Press, 1951.

Fosdick, Harry Emerson. *A Book of Public Prayers.* New

York: Harper & Brothers, 1959.

Harkness, Georgia. *Be Still and Know*. Nashville: Abingon-Cokesbury Press, 1953.

Kierkegaard, Sören. *The Prayers of Kierkegaard*. Chicago: University of Chicago Press, 1956.

Kloss, Sarah. *Prayers: Alone Together*. Philadelphia: Fortress Press, 1970.

MacGregor, J. Geddes. *So Help Me God: A Calendar of Quick Prayers for Half-Skeptics*. New York: Morehouse-Barlow, 1970.

Noyes, Morgan Phelps, ed. *Prayers for Services*. New York: Charles Scribner's Sons, 1934.

A complete bibliography on either books about prayer, or books of prayer, would be too lengthy to include. Most of the books listed are still in print. However, some older books now out of print have great value. We have included a few because they have been helpful to us. There are many more we did not include. By consulting the card catalogue of the library, especially a theological school library, many of these titles can be located. Also, most pastors have a section in their personal libraries on the subject of prayer and might make them available to a group who wished to use them for this purpose.